Pain Produces Triumph

OVERCOME FEELINGS OF HURT TO
ESTABLISH SUCCESSFUL RELATIONSHIPS

LaCarrie K. Ojong

Copyright © 2021 by **LaCarrie K. Ojong**

All rights reserved. No part of this publication may be reproduced, distributed or transmitted in any form or by any means, including photocopying, recording, or other electronic or mechanical methods, without the prior written permission of the publisher, except in the case of brief quotations embodied in critical reviews and certain other noncommercial uses permitted by copyright law. For permission requests, write to the publisher, addressed "Attention: Permissions Coordinator," at the address below.

LaCarrie K. Ojong/Rejoice Essential Publishing

PO BOX 512

Effingham, SC 29541

www.republishing.org

Unless otherwise indicated, scripture is taken from the King James Version.'

Pain Produces Triumph/LaCarrie K. Ojong

ISBN-13: 978-1-952312-76-2
Library of Congress Control: 2021911164

Dedication

I DEDICATE THIS BOOK, FIRST and foremost, to my heavenly Father in the name of His Son Jesus Christ. Thank You for giving me the strength, courage, and clarity to complete this body of work for Your glory.

I also want to dedicate this book to all those who want to find peace through healing from years of suffering from emotions containing hurt and disappointment. I was personally inspired by a genuine desire to build victorious relationships that would stand the test of time. Through the power of the Holy Spirit, I was able to receive revelation concerning the core reasons for feelings of failure in this area of my life.

I pray the methods utilized in this book will spark numerous ideas that provide effective resources for processing hurt feelings. It is my sincere hope that you obtain permanent resolutions to achieve success in your relationships. God bless you abundantly and triumphantly!

TABLE OF CONTENTS

FOREWORD..ix
INTRODUCTION..1
CHAPTER 1:   Overcome Hurt Feelings Through
               Writing Letters..5
               Dear Present Mom.....................................5
               Dear Absent Dad.....................................11
               Dear Childhood Best Friend................14
               Dear Former Boyfriend/Fiancé............18
               Dear Self..24
CHAPTER 2:   Overcome Hurt Feelings Through
               Supplication of Prayers........................47
CHAPTER 3:   Overcome Hurt Feelings Through
               Poetic Expression..................................56
               If You Really Cared...............................56
               I'm Tired..57
               A Powerful Emotion..............................58
               Betrayal...59
               The Love I Want....................................60
               Though I'm Not Perfect.......................61
               Is It Her Or Is It Me?............................62
               Lost Soul..63
               A Little Secret..64
               Who am I?...66
CHAPTER 4:   Overcome Hurt Feelings Through
               Self-Reflection.......................................69
               Conclusion..81

ABOUT THE AUTHOR..84

Foreword

*P*AIN PRODUCES TRIUMPH: OVERCOME *Feelings of Hurt to Establish Successful Relationships* by LaCarrie K. Ojong is a unique deliverance approach. She is very transparent about her flaws, shortcomings, pain, and insecurities. She takes us on a journey of the life lessons she gained and we can learn from her mistakes, so we don't have to repeat them. This book can mentor you in your relationships. I admire LaCarrie's boldness to write letters to people in her life. We gain revelation of how to overcome various issues to become better in how we treat others. Writing is very therapeutic for the soul, so the letter approach is a brilliant idea. As you read each page, you will receive healing for your own relationships. Let's face it. There will always be challenges in relationships. There are many broken relationships in ministry, business, families, etc. God has given us the ministry of reconciliation and we can no longer blame others for our part in the relationship. LaCarrie will show you how to approach each relationship maturely so you can heal and overcome setbacks and disappointments. Get ready to experience God's love and encouragement as you delve into this book.

— Kimberly Moses

Introduction

I WANT TO START OFF with a disclaimer that indicates my romantic experience described in this book was before I accepted Jesus Christ as my Lord and Savior. Now that I have the formalities out of the way, I can move on to explain my purpose for writing this book. This is not the type of reading material that meticulously lists how-to get something done or suggest following one thousand steps to receive certain results. Those techniques are great, but I needed practical applications that were personal and unique to me. I genuinely wanted to succeed in relationships, and I wanted to know from my heavenly Father why I was coming up short in this area of my life. This process started with seeking Him for answers through reading His word in the Bible on the reference of relationships, and then I asked Him in prayer to elaborate on how I could apply His word to my life. There is not anyone on this earth that knows me or the people who I chose to be in relationship with better than Father God. I am very persistent, so when my mind is made up to do something, it is super difficult to stop me from getting it done. In the past, I was often bored and impatient, which catapulted me into deep trouble because I mostly concentrated on things that were not impor-

tant. I realize now that I was too focused on what I was missing in relationships which led to the unnecessary feelings of sorrow and pain instead of focusing on the skills I needed to build and sustain successful relationships.

It was Maya Angelou that stated, "I've learned that people will forget what you said, people will forget what you did, but people will never forget how you made them feel." What I finally understood from her quote is that I undeniably possess the power to control the outcome of how people make me feel. I can recall on several occasions when I made an idiotic decision based on a feeling of frustration. That uncomfortable emotion has often led me to make hasty decisions. Even Cain murdered Abel in the Bible out of emotions of jealousy and anger because Father God favored Abel's sacrificial offering to Him over the offering of Cain. People are currently paying a lifetime price for temporary feelings that led to permanent consequences. Love ones are getting the silent treatment now due to emotions that can be managed with proper coping skills.

I decided to go on a healing journey because I could not spend the rest of my life being manipulated by my emotions. I had to discover what was holding me back from attaining beneficial and fulfilling relationships in my life. I wanted to know why I was subconsciously sabotaging my chances of achieving success in this area. I was dedicated to finding the issues causing me to get the same undesirable results. It became clear I needed to make imperative changes to position myself to receive the blessings incorporated in my heavenly Father's original purpose for relationships.

Introduction

We all have a mandate authorized by Jesus Christ to help each other triumph over trials and tribulations (Philippians 2:3-4 NKJV). However, some people are not yielding to this directive. I recognize that all relationships are not destined to last a lifetime, and I must get better at discerning the reasons and seasons for the connection. It is a proven fact that two cannot walk together unless they agree (2nd Corinthians 6:14). If a person determines that I am a season option for them, but I have decided that they are a lifetime choice for me, then we have a major problem. I have learned the harsh truth that I attract who I truly am inside. Eventually, my relationships become a summary of my negligence to focus on healing my internal nature. It is my responsibility to become a healthier version of myself through self-reflection, which gives me the knowledge that I need to seek continual growth.

I finally realized that Father God is the originator of relationships and if I wanted to overcome defeat in this area of my life, then I had to go to the primary Source. I diligently sought my heavenly Father for answers, and He faithfully gave me proactive solutions. When I prayed to Him about people that hurt my feelings, He would politely direct the conversation back toward me. This gave me the chance to fully examine my own actions in the matter, and to begin work on strengthening my imperfections. It revealed to me that everyone has room to improve, and Father God corrects His children to extract the absolute best out of us. He opened my eyes to identify a lie of the enemy that I would be labeled selfish for focusing on myself, which is not true unless I constantly exalt my wants and needs above others. Through His peace and wisdom, I am given the ability to move mountains that dare to stand in my way.

I believe the relationships mentioned in this book contributed to my core foundation for building relationships. These encounters framed my mindset on how to develop and maintain close connections. I had to allow Father God to uncover the internal issues within me so I could be transformed by the renewing of my mind through reading His word (Romans 12:2). I kept speaking its authority over my circumstances to release its mighty power in my life.

The action of processing my thoughts and feelings through letters, poems, prayers, and self-evaluation gave me the opportunity to analyze my most intimate struggles in relationships. I was determined to change the trajectory of my track record to provide more favorable outcomes. This included trusting Father God with the process of becoming an overcomer in my healing journey. I had to make a crucial decision that I would not remain a slave in bondage to my emotions anymore. We are more than conquerors through Him that loved us (Romans 8:37), so I must accept the invitation to walk boldly in His promise to have life more abundantly (John 10:10).

CHAPTER 1

Overcome Hurt Feelings Through Writing Letters

Dear Present Mom,

You raised me as a single mother. I know it was not planned because you told me that you and my father were married when I was conceived. You said that you left him when you were pregnant with me, which eventually led you to the decision of getting a divorce. This resulted in me growing up without my biological father in the household, or even present in my life. It seemed strange that I barely noticed that he was absent from the family dynamic. I know now that it was because I entirely looked to you as my ideal role model.

I completely leaned on you to tell me and show me the identity that I was supposed to become based on your measure of standards. I wanted you to fill in the missing puzzle pieces of my existence, so I placed a hefty expectation upon you. I know it was totally unfair, but you were the only parental figure in my life that I could identify as an intricate part of me. I wanted to be your mini-image, and I eagerly anticipated growing up to be just like you.

After all, you are a female. I am a female. You are pretty. I wanted to be pretty. You are independent and a working woman. I wanted to be independent and a working woman. You are a mother. I planned one day in the future to be a mother. You are strong. I desired to be strong. You are opinionated with thoughts of right and wrong. I also wanted to stand up for what I believed in with just as much courage and passion. You are my superhero. I hoped that I would be able to provide for my children with the same inspiration. You fought to be heard, which was sometimes not in the most peaceful way. I needed to be heard, but I decided from observing you that I needed to take a more diplomatic approach. I did not always agree with how you handled things, but I still yearned to learn from your teachings.

I had high expectations on the amount of time that you needed to spend with me. After all, I am your daughter, and I felt entitled to soak up your presence. I wanted all your attention so you could pour into me your knowledge and wisdom from life experiences. I realized that I was selfish because I wanted your entire focus to be on me, your eldest child and only daughter. However, it seemed that you were more preoccupied with having fun (happy, laughing, joking, having a good time) in your adult relationships to give me the time of day. I was extremely angry with you because I felt I was constantly experiencing the stern, strict, and tough side of your personality. You would yell so much at me that it caused an emotional shutdown while putting a strain on my communication with you.

Yet, I thought I could protect you from unhealthy romantic relationships, so I chose to act out in several aggressive ways. I did not know how to properly communicate my concerns to you which left me feeling helpless. I saw you enter relationships that did not have your best interest at heart because you had a strong desire to follow the matrimonial blueprint of your parents. You were raised in a two-parent household and wanted to give your children the same opportunity. I tried to get you to listen to me in my own childish way, but it was obvious that you only wanted me to be seen and not really heard. I understand now that you could not bridge the gap for having an adult to child conversation due to not having an open dialogue with your parents.

I was constantly looking for new ways to seek your approval. I remember you describing what you thought was a favorable body shape for a woman. I know it was based on your own body type prior to having children, and I wanted a physique just like yours. I would see pictures of your narrow shoulders, but I had wider shoulders. I wanted your petite chest but I had a larger chest, your flat stomach but I had a pudgy stomach, your small waist but I had a fuller waist. I saw your wide hips which I did receive, your protruding backside which was not passed down to me, and your big legs which I received as well. Two out of the seven characteristics was not a very reassuring statistic, and I felt as though I could not even measure up to your appearance standards.

Pain Produces Triumph

You would tell me to wear a girdle to help form my shape, but I did not see you taking your own advice. I decided not to listen to you because you took a 'do as I say and not as I do' approach. I often wondered what I had to do to make you proud of me. I was determined to be a daughter that gave you ample bragging rights. I tried to compliment you on your appearance often so I could get the same flattery in return. I was trying my hardest to figure out what I could say or do to gain your praise.

You commented that I was smart, so I attempted to get the best grades. You made a remark that I could run fast like my father, who was on the track team, so I joined track and field. You mentioned that my uncle was a good basketball player, so I participated through my sophomore year of high school. I never stayed interested in any of these things because you were not there to support me at any of the school events. You had to work to provide for your three children, but all I could see is that you were not there to encourage me.

I can remember pondering why you had more children. It was bad enough that you barely had time for me. Now I had to take on the responsibility as the oldest child and babysit my siblings when you were at work. There were many times that I missed out on having fun with my peers because I was stuck in the house due to my chronological placement of birth. Those babysitting experiences shaped my young mind frame into thinking that having children would be too much of a burden on me, and I would frequently say that I wanted to wait until I was less selfish to bring another life into this world. I wanted my freedom, but I was not fully equipped with the essential tools to make that a reality. I ended up having my son at 21 years old, which cut my liberty in adulthood severely.

During my preteen and teenage years, I wanted to reconnect with you to build a cordial relationship. I approached you with a question because I was having trouble in school with my peers spreading rumors about me. I was expecting you to have my back by responding to me in a way that made me feel validated and secure. I wanted to understand why this was happening to me, and I was looking to you for answers. However, I left that conversation with a feeling of being accused of doing something wrong instead of you comforting and defending me.

I was already on the offense towards you for not receiving what I felt like I needed from you. That spirit of offense triggered me to look for bad behaviors in you so I could protect myself from allowing you to hurt me again. In my adolescent mind, I was making one last effort to build solid trust and a line of communication that was open between us. I decided at that very moment I was going to stop trying to have a close relationship with you and search out your approval. I shifted my focus to hanging out with friends my age while trying to depend on their support. I learned very quickly that if I wanted you to grant me access to participate in fun activities outside the house, I had to go over and beyond performing chores that were not expected of me inside the house. This arrangement between us caused me to adopt the attitude that I got what I wanted when I decided I wanted it. I had this misconception in relationships that I always got back the reward I wanted automatically for the effort I put into maintaining it.

You never really talked to me about sex either. The only times you ever mentioned it was when you said very directly without explanation, do not engage in it. I do not even remember you giving me an instruction to wait until marriage. I did not respect your opinion because I could not understand why you would tell me to do things that you were not adhering to yourself. It was obvious that I needed more information and guidance on a serious topic such as sex, but my confidence in you on what behaviors were considered right and wrong decreased significantly. I looked to my circle of friends for direction with these matters, but that was a huge mistake. They were just as misinformed and clueless as me, which led to disastrous choices.

I was young and confused. Yet, I felt as though I knew what it took to build healthy relationships. I found out very soon that my self-reliant theories on relationships were very flawed. I could not expect people to do the same exact thing for me that I did for them. I realized that I was not going to get what I felt I needed from others just because I demanded it with my actions or words. I needed to adopt better communication skills to express my wants and needs so I could give people the opportunity to accept or deny my request. It was unrealistic to expect others to guess these things as an indication that they cared about me.

Overcome Hurt Feelings Through Writing Letters

I am pleased to say that you and I have a much better relationship now. We were able to apologize to each other for the painful things we said and did to one another over the years. Our relationship is not perfect, but we have moved past our feelings of hurt to build a closer connection. Thank you for providing me with the essential needs such as housing, food, clean water, and clothing. I have a new-found respect for you regarding the sacrifices you made as a single mother, especially now that I am one myself. I honor you as the woman who gave me life, and I am grateful that we have opportunities to make new memories together now.

Sincerely, Delivered Daughter

P.S. I decree and declare that finding the truth in my identity through Jesus Christ has delivered me from feelings of insecurity, bitterness, and disappointment.

Dear Absent Dad,

I did not learn your full name from you, which is quite disheartening in my opinion. I had to read the letters on my birth certificate, and hear the words be spoken out of my mother's mouth. I have seen a few photos of you in your younger years, but it is incredibly sad to think that I would not recognize you if I saw you on the street tomorrow. I can count on one hand the amount of your relatives that I know from Facebook connections. However, I have not seen you since I was a toddler, or formally met any of your immediate family in person.

I know that you were born in Nigeria and came to America with the objective to gain a college degree. I believe it was always your plan to go back to your home country because of your major in agriculture. I think you wanted to take those skills back to your native land to build there. Now you are living back in Nigeria, and I do not have a concrete way to communicate with you. When I have attempted to reach out over the phone in the past, I am mostly met with a busy signal on the other end. I remember wasting my money on a calling card one time just to make direct contact, but I was not able to get through to speak with you.

I wanted to hear your side of the story on what happened between you and my mother. I had asked her in previous conversations if she ever considered the possibility that you wanted to move back to Africa after completing school before she decided to marry you. I can tell from her response that she did not give it a serious thought which I think is very irresponsible and selfish on her part. I know she would not have wanted to permanently live several thousands of miles away from her family, which is understandable. It takes two to make a thing go wrong, and you also have a vital role to play in your disappearing act once the marriage dissolved.

Overcome Hurt Feelings Through Writing Letters

I am still not totally clear on the whole story, but I guess your student visa expired after the marriage ended. It is very disturbing to have only spoken with you three times on the phone in my adult life, and I still do not know you as a person. I hear you had two children prior to my birth in the United States while moving on to have four more after me in Nigeria. I do not know any of my six siblings from your offspring. I do not know your Nigerian culture, or any Nigerian traditions that you could have shared with me through my developmental years.

I could have studied and immersed myself with Nigerian culture to chase a paternal side of me that I did not know, but it would not have really seemed authentic to me. Besides every family and individual is different in the way they navigate everyday life, and I would have gotten to experience it through your personal point of view. That is the exact reason that I do not appreciate when people around me speak up or defend me about negative perceptions of African people. I do not know enough about my Nigerian heritage to have the confidence to have a clever rebuttal for their careless banter or inconsiderate criticism.

I often wonder if I have the proper knowledge to know who I am as an individual because your family tree was missing from the equation. I used to deny that my father originated from Nigeria out of shame and ignorance. I could have been proud of my Nigerian ancestry growing up if given the encouragement to accept it. However, your lack of influence in my life led me to shy away from acknowledging its existence. I am finally embracing my half Nigerian side and answering people with an enthusiastic attitude when asked about the origin of my last name. It took some time to reevaluate my integrity to get here, but I have received perfect peace for the genetics that were given to me.

I am not upset with you, and I still want to meet you someday. It would have been nice to experience a personal relationship with you while I was growing up. I could have made a side-by-side comparison of your personality traits with my own. It is intriguing to explore where I got certain characteristics in my DNA from each of my parents. Hopefully, we will get to speak on the phone again one day soon or meet face to face, but until then, I look forward to forming a close connection with you before either of us depart this world.

Sincerely, Chosen Child

P.S. I decree and declare that being chosen by Father God to be adopted in His royal family has freed me from feelings of insignificance, abandonment, and incompleteness.

Dear Childhood Best Friend,

I take full responsibility for our failed relationship. I can confess that now with greater understanding and maturity. I played a huge role in the reason our friendship does not exist any longer because I met you in a wounded space. I didn't even know who I was as a person, especially being a moody and self-indulgent teenager who thought she knew exactly what she wanted out of life. I did not have a clue, and I was moving in a dark hole of offense while focusing on what my mother was not providing me on a supportive level.

I became very selfish and unaware of the damage I was inflicting on people while building a foundation in my friendships. I only concentrated on the fun aspects of hanging out which was going to school dances, parties, and teenage clubs with friends. I did not consider the deeper emotional support that is needed to construct a solid and healthy relationship. I was too concerned with appearing cool to others instead of trying to figure out how to mend my shattered heart. I know now that we set ourselves up to fail in relationships when we attract or pursue others from a deep-seated root of unforgiveness, brokenness, resentfulness, and woundedness.

I would just move forward to meet the next person without first evaluating the negative impact relationships were having on my emotional wellbeing. I was the common denominator in these situations, and I did not realize that I was hungrily taking to offset deficits and fill voids in my life. I envied the compliments my mother gave you about your physical features and singing voice. I did appreciate your vocal abilities while harmonizing together to mimic different singing groups, but I often wondered why it seemed like I could not get praise from my own mother. I felt like all I ever received from her was critiques which eventually hardened my heart. I became abnormally determined to create the type of relationships that were going to give me what I needed at that time in my life.

We both did not know how to communicate effectively, and we both allowed outside voices to put a strain on our friendship. I was not able to fully express myself through thoughts and feelings because I buried them deep inside to protect myself from the fear of not being truly accepted and understood by anyone. My trust was never entirely given to those I called friends, and I know it is due to the superficial way I built relationships through my defensive brokenness.

I tried to put a demand on how I wanted you to be my friend. If I did something a certain way to show you that I was a good friend to keep around, then I expected you to return the same exact action back to me. I cheer you up one day when you have the blues. Then you cheer me up the next time I need some uplifting words. I recognize now when a person does not return an inspirational moment back to you, then they just did not have the capacity to provide empowering, enriching, and enlightening insight into your situation. That does not make them a bad person, but I was looking in the wrong place for comfort when I should have been seeking Father God concerning His promises to me.

I thought that if I had a boyfriend during our friendship and you did not, then I would be considerate by including you in our activities so you would not feel left out. I expected that you would do the same thing in return for me, but I felt like I was conveniently pushed to the side when the shoe was on the other foot. I felt deserted in our friendship, and I could not comprehend how a boy could come in between my best friend and me. I thought there was not anything in this world that could tear us apart, but it is evident now that neither one of us, being young, really knew what it took to sustain a close connection amongst friends.

We lost contact when you moved away while still on good terms, and I remember looking you up years later to reconnect. I got back in contact with you, and it seemed like we picked back up where we left off. Then after a while passed, I got the feeling that you did not want to be bothered anymore. I did not know what was going on in your life or even what you were going through at the time. At first, I took it personal and took it as a sign of blatant rejection. However, I had to get out of my own feelings so I could extend you the space I perceived you wanted from me. I know our friendship was not exactly pristine, but I thought we could progress to a place of more stability within our history of knowing each other. I really did not think our friendship was damaged to the point that it could not be put back together.

I have noticed that many people often want to move forward, and do not want to revisit their past friendships due to it stirring up such bad memories. There was a lot going on with us and our families during the time that we were thick as thieves. I can undeniably say that it was unusual and dysfunctional with all the moving components. I want to apologize for anything that I said or did to cause feelings of hurt and pain in your life. I want to stop the domino effect right here and right now before it collides into other people causing a pile stacked with traumatized souls. It is an endless cycle that needs to be identified so it can be strategically dismantled.

I am taking total ownership for my part in the whole ordeal because I was not mature enough to consider the consequences of my actions towards people that I called a friend. I have operated in toxic emotions of anger, hostility, and vindictiveness. I also have felt the unleashing of their vicious sting be hurled in my direction to negatively impact me. I would rather walk in blessings rather than curses to show the Father God that I serve is at work in my heart. Thank you for being my friend during a very confusing and misguided time in my life. I wish you nothing less than pure joy and abundant peace from now until forevermore.

Sincerely, Forgiven Friend

P.S. I decree and declare that feelings of inadequacy, invisibility, and rejection are torn off my life because I have a heavenly Father that has graciously forgiven me.

Dear Former Boyfriend/Fiancé,

Hindsight is certainly 20/20 when I reflect on the past circumstances that I experienced during our relationship. Our involvement caused me to question my self-esteem on many levels, and I remember contemplating if I was ever going to be a great wife to any possible future husband. I believe now that we should have never been a couple. We were both too immature and naive to know the amount of work it took to build and maintain a healthy relationship. I had a straightforward black and white performance-based approach to how I should enter and sustain romantic relationships. I compared it to a job scenario, whereas when I put in the hard work and time of labor, I anticipated seeing a reward from my efforts come back to me like a paycheck.

You give me what I want then I return the favor by giving you what you want. You give me a committed relationship then I return the favor and give you sex. You give me romance by taking me out and spending time with me, then I return the favor by cooking your meals and cleaning the home that we share. You give me a child, then I return the favor by treating you like the head of the family and household. I thought I had it all figured out, and I was moving in the right direction for the vision I wanted for my life. Yes, my thinking was completely foolish and entirely wrong. Communication, understanding, and respect were key components that we were both lacking in our relationship. Neither one of us truly knew who we were individually or what we needed from one another in a partnership.

We both tried to make each other some ideal person that we made up in our heads which we clearly were both not those things. You wanted me to be Suzy the Homemaker catering to your every need. I wanted to do things for you, not feeling like

I was obligated, and I was willing to do them for you out of the kindness of my heart. I was looking at it as an act of showing you I cared, and you ruined it by making it a tedious expectation like a chore. I wanted you to be Sam the Provider. I was expecting you to work and provide for the family to secure a better lifestyle for us in the future. It quickly became clear to me that a responsibility such as consistently taking care of the major bills in the house that you volunteered to pay was not high on your priority list.

I remember singing Beyonce's song, "Upgrade U," which you thought was crazy because you were only looking at it from a materialistic viewpoint. I was referring to the mindset aspect of achieving higher aspirations in life regarding family stability. I wanted the marriage and two children with the house attached to a two-car garage being surrounded by a brown picket fence in the suburbs. I wanted to build together as a power couple and accomplish tremendous milestones in our careers. I was so dedicated to us succeeding together that I was willing to assist you in buying a car to get you started on our journey. I was looking towards the future and you were only living in the present with no real motivation to make any future plans.

I can recollect thinking what have I done? It rendered me deeply devastated. I jumped into this relationship too quickly, giving up wifely benefits on a boyfriend which is the same thing as a boy that is a friend. I was very eager to move in with you because I was trying to escape my mother's house and gain my own independence. I did not take my time to really get to know you and now I am the mother of your child with this cheap ring you gave me, claiming you wanted me to eventually be your wife. I hastily put the buggy before the horse, and I fell for the potential of all the big plans you expressed when we exchanged future endeavors. I should have held off on being in a relationship with you until you were mature and actively performing the tasks that you mentioned on your agenda. You were not even putting forth an effort when I met you, which should have been a huge red flag waving vigorously in my face saying, "do not proceed at any cost."

I have a bad habit of assuming people are going to do what I do. I make plans to do something then I make the necessary arrangements to get it completed. I expected you to do the same thing as me, and I had to learn the hard way that it does not work in this manner. I felt ashamed because here I was putting my faith and trust in a person I scarcely knew, and now I have a child with you that is depending on both of us. I must make it work in our relationship was my distorted thoughts which had manifested from a misplaced and unresolved fear. I don't even think you were physically or emotionally faithful to me for most of our relationship. I am the type of girl who admires honesty and loyalty, so cheating has always been a dealbreaker for me. It was that exact reason, and your absence of concern to build resources for the family which prompted my decision to end the relationship.

I stayed with you longer than what was healthy because I allowed my father's absence to affect my decision making of wanting our son to grow up in a household with both his parents. I was paralyzed in our relationship for five years due to the deceptive fear of failure. Fear of our son growing up with a single mother like I did. Fear of having to start over or even having the opportunity to start another relationship again. Fear of not achieving a happy, thriving relationship because I had not been able to do so thus far. Fear of wasting precious time not reaching my goal to get married by the tender age of 23, which was a lofty teenage fantasy. Finally, fear of not finding the one who I know was meant to be in my life forever. We were just two selfish people trying to force a relationship that was not working.

Our foundation was shaky from the very beginning and a house that is divided against itself cannot stand (Mark 3:25). We were both focused on the wrong things and expecting one another to conform to our idealistic views of a partner. We did not take a great length of time or perform intricate steps to develop ourselves before agreeing to be in a relationship. Since our journey, I have learned so much and plan to allow Father God to reign sovereign in choosing my future husband. I decree and declare in the atmosphere that He will get the glory for my Kingdom marriage. I know now that making a choice to commit should not be based on where I see a guy in the future, but it should be according to the fruits he is producing at that moment (John 15:4-5 ESV). A decision to move forward with someone should be given with serious thought and prayer. I know with confidence that when I have a true relationship with my heavenly Father then I am willing and obedient to accept His answer of NO. This response leads to a protective check in my spirit of unsettledness and lack of peace giving me comfort that I will not end up with the wrong person in marriage. Father God gave women a strong sense and inner knowing called intuition that detects trouble, and it is very imperative that we do not ignore it for selfish reasons.

Even though our relationship did not last the timeframe of eternity, I want to thank you for continuing to be in our son's life. He is an amazing child with a bright future, and I guess I can give you a piece of the credit for that. He does have 23 chromosomes inherited from you, so it would not be fair to take all the accolades. Besides, he absolutely gets his intelligence and good looks from me! You are a caring father and regardless of our outcome as a couple, we continue to make a deliberate effort to co-parent without drama or chaos. It is not an ideal situation, but our son gets to have a relationship with both his parents. Our son is reaping the benefits of these decisions, and I am extremely grateful for that.

Sincerely, Redeemed Romantic

P.S. I decree and declare that I am redeemed by the wonder working power that is the blood of Jesus Christ, so I do not have to be entangled with feelings of regret, shame, and unworthiness.

Pain Produces Triumph

Dear Self,

Where have you been? I have tried everything that I know to find you. I have looked for you in other people. I have made it a mission in my life at certain times to prove that you belong in various groups and situations with the wrong people. I have seen you become argumentative just to make a point that you were right so you could feel justified. I also have seen you become unusually silent to remain diplomatic for the sake of keeping the peace. I have watched you compromise your morals, integrity, and character just to have fun. I have observed you stay where you are not wanted just to have people to hang around, or engage in conversation to receive some attention. I have watched you bend over backwards and sideways to please others with the hope that they would want to stay around you.

I have noticed you conform to your environment like a chameleon so everyone would like you and deem you as the cool chick that everyone wants to get to know. I have seen you be incredibly mean with the intentions of seeking revenge on those who hurt, disrespected, and disregarded your feelings with no visible remorse. I have watched you enter relationships only for them to end abruptly while causing your heart to grow increasingly guarded from the frequent departures. You were becoming more of a burden than a blessing to others due to your unresolved internal battle with unawareness of your identity. You can no longer live from an isolated space of frustration, hurt, pain, bitterness, and disappointment because things didn't turn out the way you expected.

I must believe now that Father God has thoughts of peace and not evil towards me to give me an expected end (Jeremiah 29:11). My life is filled with the blessings of the Lord that enriches and adds no sorrow with it (Proverbs 10:22). I must walk in my God given purpose, which will be my guiding light to triumph so I can tread over serpents and scorpions, and over all the power of the enemy, and nothing shall by any means hurt me (Luke 10:19). It will allow me to remain in perfect peace when I navigate the purpose of relationships because my mind stays on Jesus (Isaiah 26:3). Everything has a timed purpose under heaven, and it also has its own season (Ecclesiastes 3:1). I need to remember that Father God is not bound or limited by the existence of time. His timeline does not have the same time frames as His mortal creations residing in this earth realm (2nd Peter 3:8-9 NKJV). His timing is not observable in seconds, minutes, hours, days, weeks, months, and years as natural lives are constrained to operate-in through foreseeable measures.

Father God can see a thousand years of generations happen in just one measly 24-hour day. My identity is in Jesus Christ, which gives me an original blueprint on how to conduct myself here in the earth domain. I need to find my purpose to bring insight into why I am here. Father God, what is my purpose? When I truly know the answer to this question, I will be too busy demonstrating it to notice anyone or anything missing from my life. I would not be so hard on myself or torture myself with toxic thoughts of inadequacies. I know I am not perfect, and I must practice extending grace to myself and others. If I find myself getting irritated because I am not doing what I said

I would do or getting preoccupied with situations that are not beneficial to my wellbeing, then I need to take a step back, re-evaluate the issue, and make substantial changes.

I cannot project my feelings onto others in their journey when their life path is not the same as mine. I must forgive myself because I am really getting mad at me for making terrible choices in relationships that resulted in devastating outcomes. Everyone handles obstacles in their lives differently, and I must allow people to be their own navigator. It is not fair for me to demand people to be someone I want in my life based on what I feel I need from them. I can make the final choice on whether I should have them in my life or not, but I cannot try to change them as a person to fix the discrepancies that I do not like within me. I must accept their true personality in our connection while avoiding stagnation to become the best version of myself. I am only hindering progression in my own journey when I am constantly distracted with mending behaviors that are out of my control.

I must stay mindful that the enemy wants me to revert to my old nature by planting corruptible seeds in my mind to tempt my new nature in Christ Jesus (Mark 4:15 NKJV). I know he does this maneuver to take me off the small and narrow path that Father God has placed before me (Matthew 7:14). However, I make the ultimate decision on whether I allow that joker to set me back with deterrence or completely stop me from accomplishing the work Father God has for me to do. I get mad at myself and not my heavenly Father when I have realized that I believed lies from the camp of the enemy. I hate liars and satan is the father of lies (John 8:44) who influences fallen angels (2nd Peter 2:4) (his minions) to perform his dirty work to deceive both believers and unbelievers. The enemy and his minions fell from heaven due to rebellion, and he is trying to take as many people as he can with him to his eternal damnation to spend an agonizing spiritual death (Revelation 20:10).

That was his chosen fate to defy Father God and deceive himself into thinking that he could exalt his throne above the Creator of all things (Isaiah 14:13). I do not feel sympathy for him or choose to be ignorant to his wicked devices (2nd Corinthians 2:11). Distractions is his middle name and Deceptions is his last name. I will not continue to be separated from the truth anymore. The power of the truth could have saved me from many occurrences of heartache, confusion, and wasted time seeking things that did not add value or cause me to produce spiritual fruits (love, joy, peace, patience, kindness, goodness, gentleness, self-control) (Galatians 5:22-23 NKJV) in my life. It is my fault that I endured such stress because I did not search for Father God's truth. This priceless truth is found in His word and it tells me that He which hath begun a good work in me will perform it until the day of Jesus Christ (Philippians 1:6). That means that it is not how I start the race that holds me back, but it is finishing His assignments in the end that will give me the victory. I do not have to be in a rush to win the race like the old fable of the hare who stopped to rest and take a nap because he started off too fast and got exhausted. He ended up losing to the tortoise who was slow and steady in the race, which gave him an advantage to never stop until it was completed.

I want to be like the tortoise slow and steady while depending on Father God every step of the way as He directs me to the finish line (Proverbs 20:24 NIV). I believe He wants to get me there in the shortest time possible so He can get the glory for what seems impossible to man (Mark 10:27 NKJV). I will let everyone know that it was not by my human strength, ability, or might but it was by the power of the Holy Spirit that dwells within me (Romans 8:11 NKJV). I am convinced that Father God wants to show up rapidly and show out radically in my life! Hallelujah! My life will prove that He is not a man that He should lie (Numbers 23:19). My life will prove that He stays faithful to His nature and word (1st John 1:5) (Jeremiah 1:12 NASB 1995). My life will prove He is the only real, active, and true living God that exists for all eternity (John 6:57 NKJV). I want to receive every resource Father God has blessed to be assigned to my life. Therefore, I must seek out what Father God says about a matter instead of accepting what the god of this world (2nd Corinthians 4:4 ESV) (satan) says, which influences the reports of society.

God says it is not good that man should be alone, so He made a woman helper for him (truth) (Genesis 2:18). Society says that men are not interested in committing to marriage anymore (lie). God says what He has joined together, let no man separate (truth) (Matthew 19:6 NKJV). Society says that over 50% of marriages end in divorce (lie). These numbers are embellished to scare people out of getting married. Society is totally against marriage because it produces better outcomes in families which pleases God. Besides, let's think about it from a scientific research standpoint which uses a limited amount of data to form a conclusion. There is not any possible way that every person who decided to get married on this planet was interviewed in this study because that would take decades to compile and complete if this specific demographic even wanted to participate. God says that finding a wife is a good thing and favor is attained on the husband (truth) (Proverbs 18:22 NKJV). Society says that your race, skin color, hair type, body shape, and age significantly decrease your chances of getting married (lie). Society evokes fear, but Father God evokes faith (2nd Timothy 1:7 NKJV). I must constantly walk-in faith, so fear does not take residence in my heart. My faith must remain bigger than any fear that tries to come upon me (Romans 12:3 NKJV). I need to believe the true report of the Lord or the fake news of society will dictate my destiny. That is why I cannot make marriage an idol any longer by turning it into a goal that I have not accomplished in my life. I must have faith that Father God will make it happen when it is the perfect time, and not allow society to coerce me to have fearful thinking that it will never take place in my future.

I can have the desire without feeling like I am running behind schedule when it does not happen in a specific timeframe. I cannot view marriage as a project that will keep me busy when I do not have anything else that seems worth my time. I should be more concerned with preparing myself to be a wife for marriage rather than planning the actual wedding day event. I have learned that many women fall in love with a fantasy of what they think the man will become in the future (dreaming based on potential) instead of the person that he displays during the getting to know each other phase. However, men are the complete opposite. They fall in love with the woman that is portrayed right in that moment. Both sexes should accept each other where they are right now, but they both must also allow room for change while creating a safe space for each other to grow. The challenge is staying on the same page during this process, and not allowing their own selfish ideologies to dictate what that path should look like in each other's lives. I just know from my own personal experience that I cannot permit romantic comedies to send me off anymore. Those movies promote naïve daydreams that men act the same way in real life as these movies. I have found myself on many occasions ugly crying at the possibility that a man out there can be overly romantic with me. I would envision him being suddenly hit with an epiphany that he cannot live another day without my intoxicating presence.

These movies are written mostly by women to tug on the heart strings of women, and it gives a portrayal of romanticism on how women want men to display their loving affection towards women. I have learned that it is not right to put unrealistic expectations on men. I must stand in faith and trust that Father God will bring my marriage to fruition in His perfect timing, and my husband will be able to speak my love language. Father God does not need my help, so I will make the decision to be obedient to His voice and follow down the path that He tells me to go. I know I will receive His promises because only He can give me the knowledge to gain access to His blessings (Proverbs 16:3 NKJV). It is very important that I do not compare my journey to other Christian sisters' journeys in Christ around me. Father God has given them an entirely different path than mine, and it will not look the same even though we both serve in the Kingdom of God.

I have learned that when Father God provides a woman with a husband, then He is providing her with assistance in her assignments that she was purposed to accomplish in the earth. The same goes for the man when he is blessed with a wife. A wife or a husband is not there to start the work or complete the work for their spouse. They are sent to help strengthen the qualities that Father God has already placed in their marriage partner (Ecclesiastes 4:9 NKJV). Marriage is the second most crucial decision that I will ever make in my life. The most important one was accepting Jesus Christ as my Lord and Savior and maintaining a covenant relationship with God the Father through the sacrifice of His Son (Romans 5:8-11 NKJV). Christ the King demonstrated the sweetest love story by giving up His earthly vessel for His bride (the church) (Ephesians 5:25-27 NKJV) so she could live with power and authority over her oppressor (Matthew 16:18-19 ESV). A man may passionately love me, but he will never be that perfect in showing his love for me.

If I find myself getting impatient with Father God in the waiting period, then I need to ask the question, why do I want to get married at this time in my life? If the answer is a selfish reason, then I need to re-evaluate my motives and accept that it is not the right time to get married. I am feeling alone. I am feeling lonely. I am feeling unloved (I want to be a wife and mother to have someone to love me). I am feeling unwanted. I am feeling unappreciated. I am feeling like I do not matter. I am feeling invisible and unnoticed. I am feeling scared that marriage will not happen for me. I am feeling financially unstable. I am feeling incomplete. I am feeling empty. I am feeling anxious and impatient. I am feeling unsure of myself. I am feeling bored. I am feeling sexually charged. These are all selfish emotions that make moving forward in a lifelong commitment such a horrible idea. I cannot spend my precious time trying to find positive attributes in others so I can attempt to make myself complete. I need to become the person with the positive attributes so I can make myself whole.

That is the exact reason why I need to be able to discern lust from love. Lust is a phony bootleg imitation of love. Just like imitation crab meat which looks like the actual thing, but it only has a lot of fluff and fillers without any nutritional benefit. The same thing goes for lust in its appearance. It appears like love which is the real thing, but it does not contain any beneficial emotional substance or produce any spiritual confirmation. It is vital to remember that Father God operates in a Spirit of love, which produces selflessness. When I encounter a guy who I feel could be the one, then I should be asking myself questions that reveal his authentic character. Does he have a purpose that benefits others more than it adds value to himself? Is he currently walking in this purpose, and can he articulate his actions well? If not, then he has not gotten past his own wants and needs or even taken the time to consider being responsible for others besides himself. Is he intentional with trying to avoid carnal sinful activities? If so, does he make a sincere effort to protect me from falling into temptation with him? Can I see evidence of spiritual fruits (Galatians 5:22-23 NKJV) manifesting from the works of his hands? If not, then his labor will only point to him maintaining a lifestyle that solely makes him look good. What type of people does he have in his friend circle? Chances are very high that he is a direct reflection of their attitudes, values, morals, and outlook on life. I can tell a lot about a guy based on the people he chooses to keep close to him. How does he treat the people that are present in his life? If he is disrespectful to them, then I will not be exempt from receiving this same rude behavior. Finally, is he a sower that contributes his resources to advancing the Kingdom of God? It can be his time, his money, his creative ideas, or any resource that helps benefit the plans of God. That also means that he should have an active prayer life so he can position himself to be used by Father God.

Now let me look at the other side of the spectrum where the enemy operates in the spirit of lust which is selfishness. If I get a yes to these questions while assessing his character, then I must quickly run for safety to my sacred refuge that is Jesus. Is he overly confident or extremely attractive to the point he uses these attributes to manipulate situations to get what he wants, especially attention from women? Does he mention wanting to accomplish high ambition goals, but he has not taken any steps to move in the direction of his vision? If he has taken some steps to reach his objective, is he complaining about the difficulty of the journey? Is he trying to have sexual relations with me before he makes me his wife? This also includes during the engagement period of marriage because this is still considered part of the courting process. I am not officially his wife until he has made vows before God to accept responsibility for the protection of my heart. Is he expecting me to act like his wife even though I am a girl that is only his friend? This includes having the title of girlfriend which is a sneaky way for him to gain more benefits with a bare minimum commitment level. Has he popped the marriage question, but he does not have a ring, or he offers a $40 retail drug store ring when he frequently spends his money on frivolous items to promote his own wellbeing? Does he live off family members or people close to him, then casually suggest moving in together to gain his independence? It is very apparent that his priorities are not aligned with a man who has genuine desires to become a husband and a father. Bye, little boy!

These are superficial and selfish tricks of the carnal ungodly man to get what he wants by pretending that he has good intentions for me, but he is simply only concerned with what he can get to benefit himself from our connection. I can tell the maturity of a male based on his response. If he throws a tantrum, then he is stuck in a child mentality. If he stops calling and texting, then he is stuck in a selfish mentality. If he tries to persuade me to go against my moral standards, then he is stuck in a manipulative mentality. I cannot take it personal by thinking something is wrong with me or I am the reason for his behavior. I need to realize that he is in a toxic space in his life that will not be conducive to building a healthy relationship with me. That is why it is exceedingly important to make sure a man completely heals from his past feelings of hurt before considering a serious relationship with him. There is not any valid reason on this God green earth that I should suffer for his neglect to resolve the damage caused by painful emotions from his past experiences. The same principle goes for me too. I cannot move into a close intimate relationship with a man until my heavy burden baggage has been carefully sorted through and strategically unpacked. It is easy to adapt a justified attitude of reckless behavior towards others when I am operating from a place of hurt.

Every situation that is encountered from that point forward becomes a "they" statement because I have not taken the time to confront the offense so I can overcome its brutal control. They hurt me so I do not care anymore. They were mean to me, so I do not have to be pleasant anymore. They totally disregarded me as a person, so I will not make a sincere effort to try anymore. These excuses are only defense mechanisms that will shield me from receiving the healthy relationships that I truly desire in my life, and delay or stop it from happening at all. I must remember that I reap what I sow (Galatians 6:7) so I cannot attain healthy relationships from distributing unhealthy habits. I will not be able to control how people act towards me, but I am able to control my reaction which allows me to keep my power. I do not want to fall victim to the vicious cycle of blaming others for my actions, so I must put my full trust in Father God to be my Protector while focusing all my energy on healing.

I have learned throughout the years that when God is precise in His instructions on who a person should marry, then He is wanting them with that certain person for a specific purpose to bring glory to His righteous name. Father God knows His children, and He knows when an individual is too stubborn to consider marrying someone beyond their own selfish desires.

I have realized that even in those very rare occasions when Father God decides to reveal a spouse to a woman, it does not give her the green light to start pursuing the man or make a public announcement.

Adam identified Eve as the one that was after his likeness because he realized that they were spiritually connected (Genesis 2:23). It is only God that can make the spiritual introduction, so He really creates spirit-mates not soulmates. He presents the woman to the man, and then it is entirely left up to the man to spiritually recognize his wife in the woman. I believe a Christian woman should not be so quick to claim spiritual recognition of a man as her husband. We as women are more susceptible to making heart decisions based on our feelings. That is why a woman can make lifetime commitment plans regarding a guy, but he has not even asked her out on a date. We can commit our hearts to a man before we ever have an actual commitment with him. Do not awaken love until the time is right (Song of Solomon 8:4 NLT) should equate to not awakening superficial emotions before it is the right time. I want him because he is handsome. I want him because he is tall. I want him because he appears to go to the gym. I want him because he seems to know Jesus. I want him because he is single. I want him because he has a good job. I want him because he lives on his own. I want him because he drives a luxury car. I want him because he wears nice clothing, and his shoes are not old like a portable CD player. I want him because he is so pleasant when he greets me. I want him because he opened the door for me when we went into the same building. I want him because he smiled at me. I want him because he had a brief conversation with me. I want him because he smells wonderful. I want him because it looks like he knows where he is going in life. How is it that Christian women know that a guy is their husband, yet they do not know anything about him beyond the shallow exterior of what their natural eyes see and their natural ears hear? The heart is deceitful above all things, and desperately wicked; who can know it? I, the LORD, search the heart, and I test the mind, even to give to each man according to his ways, according to the results of his deeds (Jeremiah 17:9-10 NASB 1995). The heart wants what it needs to conquer which subconsciously influences the thoughts of our mind. Father God must test the mind to ensure that our character and behavior are not operating from the deceptive motives of our heart.

That is why it is very important that Christian women do not get caught in the hype of "God told me who my husband is" or "God told me that is my husband". We must be excessively cautious to avoid making misguided soul connections from our selfish soulish desires. A woman does not have to sleep with a man to create this type of connection. David and Jonathan were friends in the Bible who formed a soulmate connection between them (1st Samuel 18:1). That does not mean they slept together, but they created a bond that made an imprint on both their souls. It does not have to occur at the same time from both individuals either. One person can make a soul connection with another person based on a friendship or romantic level. It can be one-sided because the enemy is crafty that way, and he can use our words to plant thoughts in our mind with the intent to persuade us to make decisions for ourselves that cause us harm (Ephesians 6:12 NKJV). That deceptive sucker may have access to our souls, but he cannot force us to do things that are against our will. Our soul is a central house containing the mind which processes information based on our thoughts and feelings, so it is not reasonable to think that most of our dreams come from Father God. Yes, He can speak to us in this way, but He does not solely rely on our dreams to communicate His final decisions for our lives. I can remember having dreams about a guy because I had romantic feelings for him. I obviously created a soul connection, but I did not allow my dreams to influence my thoughts that he was my husband. I saw myself in a wedding dress with him as my groom, and I could have easily decided that this was a message from Father God concerning my marriage to this man. However, I had to go deeper by praying and seeking His face daily for more clarity and insight. Being a loving Father, He was faithful to confirm that the guy was not the one for me. I called on my heavenly Father, and He answered me to show me great and mighty things which I did not know (Jeremiah 33:3 NKJV). The word of God has a higher spiritual authority than a dream (Isaiah 40:8 NKJV), so we as Christian women must continue to lean not on our own understanding regarding spiritual affairs.

We as Christian women must be wise as serpents, but harmless as doves (Matthew 10:16 NKJV). We cannot get caught up in the promotion of "God told me" especially when it does not align with the character of Jesus. God told me that is my husband, but the man is a walking billboard contrary to the things of God. Father God would not undermine His integrity just to ensure that His daughter will have a marriage (Malachi 3:6). God told me that is my husband, but the woman must chase the man down to get him to notice her. Father God said that it is not good that man should be alone (Genesis 2:18) so the man should be identifying and pursuing his suitable helper not the other way around. God told me that is my husband, but the man does not have any interest in serving God. Father God is jealous (Exodus 34:14 NKJV) so He would not want a woman committing to a lifetime partner that will not encourage her to spend time with Him. God told me that is my husband, but the man has not opened a Bible since the woman has known him and he does not have an active prayer life. Father God values relationships and He would not want the woman to have a man lead her spiritually without any direction from Him (1st John 3:1 NKJV). God told me that is my husband, but the man is disrespectful, and he has not sustained any healthy relationships. Father God will not place a woman in a relationship that is harmful to her emotional state because He wants her healed and whole (Isaiah 53:5 NKJV). God told me that is my husband, but all the man cares about is making money to become wealthy without benefit to others. Father God gives money as a resource to do His works so it should not be idolized for selfish intent (Proverbs 13:22 NKJV). Do not let it be a situation where the man is making illegal money because he could very well end up in jail. Father God cherishes the family unit too much to want the woman to get involved with a man that will not be around to help lead the family and raise the children (Ephesians 6:4 NKJV). God told me that is my husband, but the man is involved in a relationship with another woman which can be defined as courtship, engagement, or marriage. Father God honors covenant, and He is a God of peace and not confusion (Deuteronomy 7:9) (1st Corinthians 14:33). Even if the man is not married or involved in a romantic relationship, it does not automatically qualify him as the woman's husband. Father God could have placed that man on the woman's heart so she could stand in the gap with prayer on his behalf because He is trying to break some things off his life. That man may not have anyone else that will do it for him. Father God could be preparing that woman to grow spiritually so He can use her for His glory (1st Timothy 2:1-4 NKJV). He does not want her falling prey to witchcraft practices by blindly using familiar spirits to manipulate the situation in her favor through her own will centered prayers or making a public declaration that unknowingly causes discord and division (Romans 16:17-18 NIV). Unfortunately, I have previously fallen into this wicked trap set by the enemy. I called a man my husband when in fact he was not my God ordained spouse. Sadly, that is not Father God, and I had to quickly recognize distinct traits of the Holy Spirit who would not encourage me to speak a lie out of my mouth! Blessed are the peacemakers for they shall be called the children of God (Matthew 5:9). The Holy Spirit will never tell a woman to put a title claim on a man as her husband in a public speech without having an actual marriage. The Holy Spirit speaks the whole truth (John 16:13), and that man would not be her husband officially until after he says, "I do." We as Christian women can call those things which be not as though they were in faith (Romans 4:17) (I am a Kingdom wife, I am joyously married, I have a loving and caring husband, My husband is a God fearing man, great leader, and an avid prayer warrior), but she should not be announcing to the world or getting stuck in her heart to the point she don't want to move forward from the specific man until it is factually true. We must be very sensitive to not impose our will on the will of others or covet a man based on our feelings. God told me that is my husband, but he does not have any convictions about having sex before marriage. Father God is very clear in His word that fornication (sex outside marriage) is a sin, and it only leads to spiritual death (1st Corinthians 6:9 NKJV). Sex outside the covenant of marriage carries a tremendous amount of unnecessary emotional repercussions that some women never get over in their lifetime. God told me that is my husband, but the man does not mind living together before marriage. Father God would not approve of the woman and man flirting with the possibility of falling into temptation to sin (Matthew 26:41 NKJV). Besides, He is the ultimate Provider and King of provision. Lastly, God told me that is my husband, but the man is emotionally unavailable. Father God holds the man accountable for guarding the woman's heart, so He is not putting the woman in a situation where she does not feel loved and secure (Ephesians 5:25-27 NKJV).

The "God told me" lie is a distraction from the enemy to keep women from receiving God's whole truth in their hearts and to keep women angry with God due to the fact they are too focused on not being a wife. It makes them more vulnerable to making the wrong decisions for a life partner when it does not happen fast enough for them. Father God does not operate in telling half-truths because that would make Him a liar. God does not want to deceive us in any way, so He is going to give us the entire truth. He is not going to tell us anything that would contradict His word or compromise His integrity (1st John 1:6 NKJV). We as Christian women also need to be mindful that the enemy loves to recycle the old to make it look new. We cannot be so willing to go back to entertaining an ex. They are an ex for a reason, and since I have found Christ then the old things have passed away in my life (2nd Corinthians 5:17). I must remember that I can make anything look good in my sight if I try hard enough especially when I am feeling great. That ex may look changed from the outside, but there is not any heart change in the inner man. It is easy for a man to fix the outer appearance to make it look appealing, but it is only Father God that transforms the heart of a man from the inside that then pours out to others (2nd Corinthians 3:18 NKJV). I must keep reminding myself that Father God will do a new thing according to His word (Isaiah 43:19). It is the two people who He has joined together to never separate (Mark 10:9 NKJV) that bring about His glory. I must believe that He wants me to succeed in this area of my life so if I do not have it right now then it is not my time to have it yet.

I have learned to remain in peace when I get a definitive NO from Father God on something I asked Him because I really wanted it. He proves to have something better for me in the end that will not give me a heavy burden of stress, and it allows me to rest in His goodness. A job may seem appealing financially, but that does not mean it is healthy for my mental state. All money is not good money to earn, and if it is loved too much then it is considered the root of all evil (1st Timothy 6:10). That leads to doing whatever it takes to get it in your grasp including selling your soul and body for profit. I need to trust that Father God knows best for my life, and I must get it deep down in my heart that He is the only one who knows the perfect time to release His blessings to me. He loves me enough to give it to me when I am ready for it. For all the promises of God in Him are yes, and in Him amen to the glory of God through us (2nd Corinthians 1:20). I am grateful that my heavenly Father wants to see me triumph and prosper in my life. I cannot do that when I decide to move in a direction without Him or I chose to give up. That is what the enemy wants me to do, but I refuse to let him defeat me. That deceitful bully will not cause me to fail and miss out on all the blessings that Father God has promised me. That thief must restore sevenfold what he stole when his hand is caught in the "blessings" jar (Proverbs 6:30-31). The enemy needs to get ready to run me all that he owes me plus some, and I am ready to receive an abundant overflow for the trouble he has caused me. What the enemy meant for evil against me, Father God has meant it for good (Genesis 50:20 NASB 1995). I decree and declare in the atmosphere that it is my time to reap a harvest in due season if I do not give up (Galatians 6:9 ESV).

I think back over my past career choices, and how I always had this feeling that I was supposed to find my career in healthcare. I did not have a clue when I graduated from high school what area of healthcare that I was going to find a job. Nursing was one of the careers I considered pursuing at the time, but I was not completely confident that was the direction I should go. I wanted to perform research, so I asked people in the nursing field if it was a good choice to make. I remembered feeling discouraged because I was continually hearing negative feedback, and any positive feedback I heard was not enough to motivate me to move forward. I allowed fear to change my course of action in obtaining nursing as my career choice, and I decided to go with another position in the healthcare field. Father

God wanted the children of Israel to possess the land He promised them immediately, but they got delayed due to doubt and disobedience. They were setback 40 years and lost in a desolate place because they accepted a bad report that caused hesitation to move forward in where God was wanting to take them (Joshua 5:6 NKJV). However, our stories differ in the reason for the delay. I had a late start in my calling of nursing due to lack of understanding, wisdom, and immaturity. I did not know at that time in my life how to seek Father God for guidance on what direction I needed to take in the healthcare industry. I had a strong feeling it was that field, but I did not have a destination point. Since that uncertainty in my position selection, I have learned that when Father God wants me to do a specific task, then He will give me concise instructions to complete it. I believe it was not my timing to enter the nursing field after high school, and Father God allowed me to go in a different direction in the healthcare field because I was not mature enough to receive the blessing. I know now that if I had entered a nursing position at that time in my life, then I would have ended up in the wrong specialty, wrong position, or just quitting all together. I would have messed it up big time, and I believe in my heart that Father God saved me from myself. He delivered me from making my own plans and moving in my own direction in life that would have led me to being miserable with my choices. Thank You, heavenly Father, for protecting me even when I did not have the capability of seeking You for the correct answers in my life.

Now I am entering the nursing field later in my journey because Father God never changed His plans on what He wanted me to do. I know now that I am exactly where Father God wants me in these fresh seasons purposed under heaven (Ecclesiastes 3:1). Through my transition period, I sought Him for guidance and direction because I was open to the changes He wanted to make in my life. I was ready to receive His specific instructions from a more mature perspective so I could follow His promptings without getting distracted and moving off course. I am right where I need to be in His perfect timing (Acts 1:7 NKJV). I know in my heart from my experiences that Father God truly knows the end from the beginning (Isaiah 46:10). He is Alpha and Omega (Revelation 22:13 NKJV), and time is an infinite part of His existence. I think about all the times that I was not seeking His face, and how His grace rescued me from a life of destruction. I am thankful to Father God for a praying maternal grandmother who knew the power of prayer. Intercessory prayer is essential for asking heavenly Father to intervene on the behalf of those who do not have the strength or knowledge to do it on their own. I must have a prayer life to accomplish the works Father God has planned for me to do in the earth. I would not be here today fulfilling my purpose if it were not for the effectual and fervent prayers of the righteous that availeth much (James 5:16). I pray that I can continue the legacy of prayer in my bloodline so my family generations can benefit from God's protection. Father God is LOVE (1st John 4:16) and I plan to showcase the greatest commandment of all (Matthew 22:37-38 NLT) everywhere I am blessed to set foot. To God be the glory forever and always!

Sincerely, Surrendered Soul

P.S. I decree and declare that my soul is surrendered to the High Priest that is Jesus Christ so I can be transformed from feelings of pride, selfishness, and discontentment.

CHAPTER 2

Overcome Hurt Feelings Through Supplication of Prayers

FATHER GOD, IN THE mighty name of Jesus. Thank You, Father God, for helping me to not be blinded by unforgiveness or constantly looking through the lens of disappointment. Thank You, Father God, for assisting me to trade beauty for ashes (Isaiah 61:3) and focusing on all the wonderful blessings I presently contain in my life. It does not matter if these things are deemed small to many people because I know that it is Your almighty hand giving me Your splendid portion. Thank You, Father God, for making me ruler over little with an expectation that I will prepare to be ruler over much (Matthew 25:23 NKJV). I cast down every imagination that tries to exalt itself against the knowledge of You (2nd Corinthians 10:5 NKJV) or wants to attempt me to walk in frustration wrapped up tightly in anger, so I am not able to receive the love that You have ordained for me through the foundations of the world. Thank You, Father God, for giving me the strength to dispense mercy and grace towards others as I openly welcome Your generous distribution of mercy and grace towards us. I pray to quickly recognize when I am trying to control circumstances that affect people around me instead of allowing You to mold me into a leader that teaches by example through actions rather than sound like a clanging cymbal. Thank You, Father God, for providing me with the courage to not put superficial bandages on my wounds, and for giving me a word of knowledge to create an atmosphere that promotes healing for a full recovery. I will sever the spirit of offense at the root so it will not damage my heart or the hearts of those who I encounter in my lifetime. Thank You, Father God, for supplying me with a forgiving spirit such as Joseph in the Bible who was originally thrown in a pit to die, but then was later sold into slavery from those same family members. I must clothe myself in the spirit of righteousness just as Joseph did when he was going through difficult times without any signs of relief. He could have effortlessly adopted the spirit of offense and bitterness towards the ones that totally disregarded his life. Yet, Joseph stayed humble and submitted to God who was able to use him to be a blessing to thousands of people including those same family members that abused him. Thank You, Father God, for draining offense and bitterness from my heart so I can be used to bring glory to Your Holy name. I cannot dictate the actions of others, but I can dictate how I respond, react, and what I allow to penetrate as well as live in the depths of my heart. Thank You, Father God, for planting a word of wisdom in my spirit that eradicates me from taking the poison of offense, unforgiveness, and bitterness into relationships to release a slow spiritual death because wounded people carry the effects of their emotions like an infectious disease. I do not want to be toxic from my feelings of hurt so I can freely do Your will without any barriers holding me back from fulfilling Your plans and purpose for my life. Thank You, Father God, for showing me the wicked devices of the enemy to keep me bound with ignorance and unable to receive all the blessings You have spoken over my life. The enemy (a cunning and conniving thief) comes to kill my joy, steal my peace, and destroy my righteousness in the Holy Ghost (Romans 14:17), but You, heavenly Father, have come to give me the powerful Kingdom of abundant life (John 10:10). I vow to love and serve You with my whole heart for now until forevermore. Amen.

*F*ATHER GOD, IN THE mighty name of Jesus. Thank You, Father God for showing me where I have open doors for the enemy to come in like a flood and cause detrimental chaos in my relationships. The Spirit of the Lord will lift-up a standard against him (Isaiah 59:19) and close those doors with His love and truth. Thank You, Father God, for supplying me with the wisdom and understanding to triumph in building beneficial connections through relationships. I trust that You will help me to remove demanding behaviors that attempt to pull out of people what I need from them so I can allow them to demonstrate their true nature without any hidden expectations from me. Furthermore, I cannot put an entitled attitude on the need for You, Father God to prove the manifestations of Your word, but I must believe with tremendous faith that You will deliver on Your promises. Thank You, Father God, for filling any voids, deficits, and missing character-building qualities that cause me to take from others as a burden instead of exceedingly giving to others as a blessing. Please reveal to me strategies on how to cast down the lies of the enemy stating that I am not good enough or I do not have the right resources. Heavenly Father help me bring into captivity every thought telling me that I am equipped by You with abundance, and I am not lacking anything. Those who hunger and thirst for Your righteousness shall be filled (Matthew 5:6) so I undoubtedly believe that once I drink from Your endless well that cannot run dry then I will never feel the sensation of thirst again (John 4:14). Thank You, Father God, for teaching me how to sustain a close relationship with You while learning to represent Your presence of light and goodness to others. I want to be the best version of myself and inspire others to reach the same goal. I do not want to focus on wrong behaviors directed towards me, but I want to discern the reasons and seasons people are in my life as an opportunity to grow in my own journey. For Your ways heavenly Father are higher than our ways, and Your thoughts are higher than our thoughts (Isaiah 55:8) which makes Your plans and purpose for my life never changing. You can swiftly exchange evil for good, and You can faithfully bind up the wounds of the brokenhearted (Psalm 147:3 NKJV). I pray that I can stop the deadly cycle of toxic relationships so I can nurture an environment of internal healing. Thank You, Father God, for opening my spiritual eyes to see past the surface of a person to acknowledge and appreciate their strengths. I want to see people as You see people, heavenly Father, to assist them on their purposed journey rather than hinder their potential growth. I do not want to lean on my own understanding when it comes to building successful relationships. I must trust Your advice because You are far from the shadow of turning (James 1:17) while continuing to remain the same yesterday, today, and forevermore (Hebrews 13:8). Thank You, Father God, for correcting me in love and truth that is not done for condemnation, but to instruct and guide me into the victory already won on cavalry by the blood of Jesus Christ. My relationship with You is the key foundation I need to attain triumphant relationships with people I encounter in my lifetime. Thank You, Father, for answering me when I call on You, and showing me great and mighty things which I do not know (Jeremiah 33:3 NKJV) to give me the opportunity to make better choices as I walk in a better understanding of Your intended purpose for relationships. I will honor You with the fruits of the Spirit (Galatians 5:22-23 NKJV) this day forward in my relationships to bring glory to Your Holy name. Amen.

FATHER GOD, IN THE mighty name of Jesus. Thank You, Father God, for providing me with the peace to not dwell on the past or to worry about all the things that did not happen according to my plans. You want me to look forward to the future so You can distinctively mold me into Your original masterpiece to showcase the marvelous works of Your hands (Ephesians 2:10 NLT). Thank You, Father God, for protecting me from the enemy's schemes to keep me trapped in a prison of constantly looking back at what could have been or intensely focusing on what I am currently missing in my life. I am progressing forward with certainty that You are well able to do exceedingly and abundantly above all that I can ask or think according to Your Spirit's power that works in me (Ephesians 3:20 NKJV). Heavenly Father, You are everything that I need and want so I decree and declare that I am made whole by Your yoke destroying presence, and Your chain breaking anointing. Thank You, Father God, for wanting to do a new thing in my midst (Isaiah 43:19), and I do not have to carry feelings that render fear of failure in my relationships any longer. I cannot create new and alive things from old dead things, and new wine cannot be put in old wineskin or it will ruin them both (Matthew 9:17 NKJV). My past cannot be put into my future or it will taint my destiny. Thank You, Father God, that I am not paralyzed in stagnation, but I am moving full speed ahead due to Your guidance and favor. You are constantly working, and I do not want to miss out on what You are doing in these upcoming seasons of my life. Heavenly Father, You are the one and only Creator, and there is none above You in all the universe. You formed substances in the earth with a command of Your spoken words. Let there be light! (Genesis 1:3) There is not anything that is impossible for You (Luke 1:37). I decree and declare that I have the successful relationships of my desire and they encourage me to be better than the previous day before. Thank You, Father God, for supplying me with the supernatural insight to recognize when the enemy is trying to recycle an old and familiar interior without any spiritually fruitful substance into a new and attractive exterior based on outer preference. The guy can be appealing to the natural eyes on the outside, but underneath he has the same spiritually faulty foundation with a renovated floor plan of personality traits. Thank You, Father God, for showering me with Your perfect love and precious grace so I can be free from bondage concerning fear of failure in relationships. I want to serve You without any limitations because I cannot be fully utilized by You if I am operating from a space of brokenness and regret. I must position myself to receive Your blessings which makes me rich, and You add no sorrow with it (Proverbs 10:22). I need to let go of the negative emotions that are plaguing my heart. I am dedicated to shedding all this junk mail in the inbox of my heart so I can make room for the refreshing abundance of Your restoration. Amen.

*F*ATHER GOD, IN THE mighty name of Jesus. I accept the authority given to me through Christ Jesus who sacrificed His human life on the cross so I can live to walk in triumph over the enemy (Galatians 1:3-4 NKJV). He is now the King, Lord, and Savior of my very existence, and I am thankful for the protection that He provided over my life. Thank You, Father God for keeping me from permanently destroying my future all these years and preserving me through my immaturity which caused delays in my purpose, and receiving the fullness of Your promises. You have the perfect wisdom to know when it is the best time for me to receive the blessings that You mapped out for my journey (Habakkuk 2:3 NKJV). I thought I had it all figured out on my own in the past, and I was heading in the right direction. Thank You, Father God, for leading me down the path of Your perfect will through all the terrible choices that I made in my life (Proverbs 19:21 NIV). I did not know who I was, what I was specifically supposed to do, or even that I had a calling from You. I did not seek Your guidance and direction because I was completely unaware that You had a plan for my life that was greater than anything I could ever imagine. I always knew throughout my life to give You praise for the blessings I received, but I was not taught to seek Your face on the steps I needed to take to get it accomplished. Thank You, Father God, for giving me a new perspective on marriage. Everything that I desire does not have to be a goal on a to-do list and viewed like a task that needs to be completed within a specific timeframe. I can be liberated from feeling as though I am failing if I do not get it done by a certain deadline. I rebuke the lies of the enemy that I am falling behind, and there is not any possible way to catch back up. Thank You, Father God, for affording new opportunities in my life because You are not bound by the methodology of time. I can walk in confidence knowing You are releasing the blessings to me in the right seasons of my journey, and it will not be a minute too soon or too late. Heavenly Father, I am amazed at Your perfect timing which offers a recharge of strength to persevere in the presence of weary faith (Isaiah 40:31 NKJV). Thank You, Father God, that I am seeking Your assistance to complete every assignment that You have set before me to do. I will give You alone the honor and the glory for every milestone along the way because it is only by Your might and Your Spirit that I am able to achieve victory. Thank You, Father God, for being with me faithfully when I acknowledge You in all my ways so You can direct me on a straight path of righteousness towards Your promises (Proverbs 3:6). I will live by every word that proceeds out Your mouth from the Bible (Matthew 4:4 NKJV) because it is my daily portion of spiritual nourishment (Luke 11:3). It will keep me spiritually strong and healthy so I can use it as a sword to breakthrough and annihilate the lies of the enemy (Ephesians 6:17). Thank You, Father God, that I am reading Your word to see what it has to say about me and communing with Your Holy Spirit to enlighten my understanding of its power when spoken over my life. The Holy Spirit is my Helper as well as my Comforter (KJV), and He will teach me all things and bring to my remembrance everything that was said during the ministry of Jesus (John 14:26 NKJV). I want to know the Holy Spirit for myself, so I can discern and accurately identify His voice of truth from the misleading voices in the world (John 16:13). The world does not know Him (John 14:17), but I am determined to make Him my very best friend. Thank You, Father God, that You are my Shepherd, and I am your sheep that hears Your voice without following the voice of a stranger (John 10:4-5 NASB 1995). I decree and declare that I am only going to receive the truth report of the Lord, and I am asking for spiritual discernment to know when there are any deviations in its authenticity. I am blessed that You are on my side, for greater are You that is within me then he that is in the world (1st John 4:4). If You are for me then who can be against me? (Romans 8:31) I will serve You all the days of my life because You are my Maker and my Husband (Isaiah 54:5 NKJV). Amen.

CHAPTER 3

Overcome Hurt Feelings Through Poetic Expression

IF YOU REALLY CARED

You tell me that I am your one and only boo
But I do not believe that statement is sincerely true
I confess to you that I have your back and truly do care
But you continue to be absent from my life and never actually there
I need you next to my side because it feels completely right
But your lack of interest makes our relationship less strong and tight
I want to be the lady that you are proud to have on your arm
But we always argue and you are rapidly losing your charm
You act like you want to spend more time getting to know me for real
But you continue to play with me like a toy in a fast-food kiddie meal

I am constantly trying to prove to you that I am the perfect one
But you deliberately look the other way so I need to be done
If you really cared then you would unselfishly find out what to do
And I would not be pouring out my heart in this silly poem to you

I'M TIRED

I'm tired of your foul deceptive lying
I'm tired of my relentless inconsolable crying
I'm tired of these addictive thoughts of you
I'm tired of the lethal agony you put me through
I'm tired of devaluing myself to prove I honestly care
I'm tired of clinging to past memories on the times that we share
I'm tired of your weak, predictable, and unoriginal excuses
I'm tired of not having courage to walk out while holding up the deuces
I'm tired of the mental games to selectively give affection back
I'm tired of your cold and distant mind being completely off track
I'm tired of this crippling and unnecessary prolonged stress

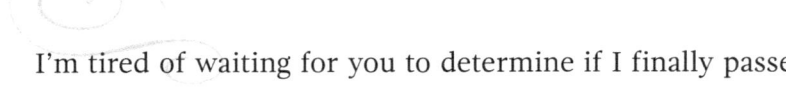

PAIN PRODUCES TRIUMPH

I'm tired of waiting for you to determine if I finally passed the test

I'm tired of your entrapment that leads to heartbreaking pain

I'm tired of feeling unloved, unappreciated, and ashamed

I'm tired of going through hoops circling around tormenting emotions

I'm tired of aiming my heart towards a target of misguided devotions

I'm tired of continuing to have hope that my love is enough for you

When I know in my heart that my departure is beyond overdue

I'm tired of exposing myself to your brutal disrespect again and again

This path is not healthy for me so this connection must permanently end

A POWERFUL EMOTION

Love is such an intoxicating and powerful emotion

Leading me under its spell of number 9 love potion

It can make me think about a person on repeat every hour

Obsessively counting minutes that we are apart like a clock tower

Is finding love really the treasure that some people think?
If you ask my opinion right now, I think love purely stinks
It gets me all wrapped up with warm and electric feelings
Blinding my common sense to not get caught in shady dealings
It gives me time to evaluate myself but do I ever locate the lesson?
Letting it teach me values and principles to receive a special blessing
If only I knew its original plan for me then I can be confident to learn
How to trust the process faithfully and patiently wait for my turn
The point I must make about love is I will not be afraid to take it slow
Earnestly praying for the person I love to have wisdom to already know
What the mysterious and alluring meaning of love is truly about
When rendering service to one another without the burden of doubt

BETRAYAL

*T*HIS DEEP AND COMPLETE emptiness I feel inside
    It is hard for me to articulate or fully describe

Pain Produces Triumph

My heart is filled with so much sadness and pain
I have to rise above my pride to break this heavy chain
I want to be a good listener and a supportive friend
But I am blinded with feelings of hurt that won't end
The heart is deceptive so who can really know its real desire?
Being fed accelerants of lies to build up a mass destructive fire
I think what I want is right for me but is it entirely true?
I don't know myself well enough to have a clear point of view
Betrayal is on the move and I am not exempt from its wrath
Feeling justified in my bitterness and traveling down a dark path
Realizing it's not fair to others if I don't work on the little girl inside me
Determined to nurture her insecurities and bring restoration to her misery
I am dedicated to succeeding in relationships so I can have great victory
Desiring to achieve better outcomes that produce greater levels of intimacy

THE LOVE I WANT

I WANT A LOVE THAT makes me vividly see
How exhilarating and joyous life can be
I want a love that lets me securely know

There is no other place that is safer to go
I want a love that takes me directly where
My heart finds peaceful rest inside there
I want a love that shows me simply how
To relinquish my past starting right now
I want a love that makes me boldly feel
That all my dreams have become real
I want a love that lets me sweetly hear
Our wedding song playing softly in my ear
I want a love that is destined to last forever
Enduring the years that we share together
This love that I want is quite possible to find
For some have found this love while I still await mine

THOUGH I'M NOT PERFECT

I MIGHT NOT HAVE THE fairest and smoothest skin
But I have unique character that is provided within
I might not have the straightest and longest hair
But I am not too conceited that I am not able to care
I might not have the lightest color shades in my eyes
But take a deeper look in mine that tell you no lies
I might not have the largest and perkiest breast
But I am not full of drama or keep up various mess
I might not have the tiniest and narrowest waist

But I can give you a love that is hard to replace

I might not have the biggest and most voluptuous backside

But a woman with her own resources won't need you for a ride

I might not have the widest and roundest hips

But your secrets will never leave my trustworthy lips

I might not have the cutest and most adorable smile

But I can promise you that I will be around for a while

Though I am not perfect, no measurable beauty standard really is

It's the warped influences of society that have people thinking like this

IS IT HER OR IS IT ME?

Is it her or is it me?

I need to know now so spill the tea!

You are telling me that she is just a friend

Or are you really admitting that you see her time and time again?

Loving me is what you are saying be on your mind

Bur our relationship has reached an emotional decline

You are running and telling her what we do when she is not around

Painting pictures that I am the crazy girlfriend that keeps you homebound

I can't take any more of this manipulation you are putting me through

If you want to be with her then this is what you need to do

Stop acting like you want to be with me and start over with that girl

Because I will not sit back and allow you to have the best of both worlds

If being with her is where you decide to belong

Keep it moving that way and leave me entirely alone

LOST SOUL

I AM LOST IN A bottomless pit as my feelings grow wings and take flight

I do not have a place for them to land or even a resting sanctuary in sight

I want to fly free as an elegant gorgeous and graceful white dove

Soaring to new heights in victory while conquering all obstacles from above

My emotions seem to render me paralyzed from progress with a captivating illusion

While my mind is trying to find logical explanations for a perfect solution

There is desperation and hurt that fills my heart with poisonous lies

Pain and sorrow that is drowning my hope through forming unhealthy ties

I need an escape plan to rescue my lost and depleted soul

From this deep pressure of bitterness that is turning my heart cold

I have to save myself with mighty strength to end this heavy despair

Weakly protecting my heart with bad strategies as it continues to lay bare

A damaged heart cannot find a lost soul hidden in depths of isolation

Without the power of healing to revive its essence from fated desolation

I must have a chance to recover parts of me that seem misplaced forever

As I overcome feelings of total defeat to locate precious life treasures

Now I understand that winning was the predestined conclusion beyond what my eyes can see

For my soul was created from a Higher Power that never deviated in His superior plan for me

A LITTLE SECRET

HAVE YOU EVER WANTED someone so much to be your true soulmate?

Falling head over heels fast for him while trying hard to contemplate

Will he accept my invitation to receive this tender and loving embrace?

Feeling vulnerable yet open to fill the void of my heart's incomplete space

I know he has some feelings for me but are they stronger than mine?

Wondering if he will cash out on my love or should I move to another line?

The more intimate our conversations become then the harder it gets

Fantasies invading my mind as a couple but too shy around him to admit

That I want to spend every waking moment with him that I possibly can

A vivacious soul with the right package to showcase as his woman

I finally realized that patience is the golden virtuous key

To unlock his heart and give him a fair opportunity

Hopefully he gets a clue that my love is what he needs to withhold

Or I will never reveal to him that this little secret was ever told

WHO AM I?

*T*HIS IS A DESCRIPTIVE question that will determine how I consciously move

In this earth domain where I spent many wasted years trying to prove

That I needed to seek the approval of others to give me a sense of identity

Missing out on key moments to discover the authentic core that is truly me

It's easy to write adjectives listing details to describe life's mysteries

Deemed ineffective if I am not owning the words spoken over my destiny

I am a child and a woman of the Most-High God who is made in His likeness and image to produce the fruits of the Spirit

I am strong and powerful while serving Father God with gladness to glorify Him with light that is brightly lit

I am exquisitely gorgeous and unique with intelligence by His wisdom to accept the resource of strength that supports His will as a pillar.

I am a caregiver and a friend that is blessed to be a mother who is loved by my heavenly Father as I walk in His glorious anointing of a healer

I am a mentor and an educator that uses creativity along with seeds of faith to position myself in the works of my Father's hands

I am submissive and obedient to God while exploring this life as a learner and a student that receives truth in revelation from Holy Spirit as it stands

I am a giver of grace, forgiveness, and service of myself with the ambition to understand the path of others from an empathetic perspective

I am a receiver of grace and mercy as a daughter and sister that is determined to walk in the callings and giftings of Father God's directive

I am a fervent prayer warrior with the intent to win spiritual warfare to conquer territory as a queen in the Kingdom of Light

I am beautifully and wonderfully made to use the word of God as a sword of spiritual armor for the purpose to never back down from a fight

I am a mouthpiece for the Most-High God that speaks an abundance of prosperity over my life declaring myself the head and not the tail

I am a lender to many nations that is seated in heavenly places with Jesus to fulfill the Father's business by sharing the good news in priority mail

I am an entrepreneur that has a multi-billion-dollar budget that clothes the naked, shelters the homeless, and all things according to the Father's will

I am a visionary and a world-changer that sets trends by speaking the word of God and waiting for heavenly instructions while quietly still

I am a Kingdom bride by spiritual birthright and a royal heir with Christ having the faith of an avocado seed that solely depends on the Most-High

I am caring and genuinely sensitive to not think I have fully arrived as I will always be a work in progress forcing the old nature to completely die

I am announcing my freedom from self-doubt because it's impossible to please God without faith which is a critical point that can't be missed

I am a chosen person and a crowned priesthood set apart to bring Father God glory while equipped to triumph in adversity for such a time as this

Heavenly Father, I want my life to reflect the obedience of your word

Relying on your truthful scriptural guidance and not lies that I heard

These words that have been released will be near and dear to my heart

Your Holy Spirit breathing fire in my direction to give me a fresh start

I will walk diligently by radical faith and not by untrue misleading sight

Proclaiming things into existence through the power of God's strong and wondrous might

CHAPTER 4

Overcome Hurt Feelings Through Self-Reflection

1. Who is the first person that hurt me in a relationship? What did I do to process those hurt feelings? When did I seek or receive resolution for those hurt feelings? Why did I get hurt feelings in the first place? How can I express my hurt feelings to the individuals who hurt me in a non-accusatory or combative way?

_____
_____
_____
_____
_____
_____
_____

Pain Produces Triumph

Overcome Hurt Feelings Through Self-Reflection

2. Who has caused hurt feelings in my current relationships? What triggers from others seem to bring up hurt feelings in me? When did I realize that I am constantly experiencing reoccurred hurt feelings in my relationships? Why do I allow hurt feelings to negatively impact the way I think about the people who hurt me? How can I overcome hurt feelings in my relationships so I will not continuously live-in the pain of negative emotions?

_____

_____

_____

_____

_____

_____

_____

_____

_____

_____

_____

_____

PAIN PRODUCES TRIUMPH

3. Who have I aggressively confronted or initiated conflict with in my relationships? What happened that brought about such a strong approach from me? When did I notice that it became more about who was right or wrong? Why did I handle the impact of getting my feelings hurt in an unusual way? How could I have resolved the matter in a more peaceful manner?

_____
_____
_____
_____
_____
_____
_____
_____
_____
_____
_____
_____
_____

Pain Produces Triumph

4. Who have I reacted towards with actions of retreating, seeking revenge, or finding a resolution for my hurt feelings? What outcome did I receive from any of these methods, and did I get my desired results such as an apology? When have I ever taken the initiative to apologize first in relationships, and was I expecting it to change the behavior of the other people? Why do I have relationships in my life that did not last very long? How did the ending of those relationships affect me emotionally, and what can I do now to improve chances for longer lasting relationships in the future?

_____

_____

_____

_____

_____

_____

_____

_____

_____

_____

_____

PAIN PRODUCES TRIUMPH

5. Where are places I can go to relax (ex. gym, spa, walking/bicycling trail) or people I can talk to (therapist, pastor, godly and unbiased counselor or friend) so that I can help manage stress? How many hours out the week can I use to participate in self-care activities? Do I believe that taking care of myself will help benefit others? What are small steps that I can take each day to promote self-love?

_____
_____
_____
_____
_____
_____
_____
_____
_____
_____
_____
_____
_____

Pain Produces Triumph

6. How can I come up with creative ways to perform self-evaluations (heart checks)? How can I turn negative emotions into positive attributes within me to benefit my relationships? What are things that I can do to serve others without expecting anything in return? What goals do I want to accomplish in the process of building successful relationships?

_____

_____

_____

_____

_____

_____

_____

_____

_____

_____

_____

_____

_____

_____

_____

Pain Produces Triumph

Conclusion

*I*T IS NOT THE amount of people that are my friends that determines success in relationships, but it is the ability to maintain healthy and spiritually fruitful relationships. I have learned that I cannot completely avoid hurt feelings in relationships, and the right key to healing involves forgiveness. I can declare triumphant freedom from hurt that I have experienced in previous relationships to move forward with my life; however, first, I should take a close look at myself before building another relationship. It is important for me to decide that I am not going to foster or entertain toxic relationships any longer. Will it take work to walk through the process of my healing? Absolutely, and I am aware that there is an enemy running loose like a roaring lion seeking someone to devour (1st Peter 5:8). That evil, underhanded, and washed up former anointed cherub (Ezekiel 28:14) wants to see me stumble and fall from grace. That is his assignment which is to remove me from the protection of Father God so he can destroy my faith and trust in God or cause me to curse God to His face (God is a liar, God is not faithful, God does not care about me or the people that I love, God does not keep His promises, God is not good or even real because if He was then this or that would not have happened). The enemy did this exact thing to Job in the Bible so he would turn his back on Father God. Job was a faithful servant of God, and it was his willingness to trust God in tumultuous times that he was able to get back a double portion of everything the enemy stole from him. God knows the strength of His children, and He will not allow us to be tempted beyond what we can bear (1st Corinthians 10:13 NKJV). That is why it is very crucial to not shut down when facing opposition in life, but to instead reach out for help so we do not feel hopeless to make permanent decisions on temporary problems. There is not anyone who should be embarrassed to share their struggles because there is not any problem that only one person is going through alone. We are all here to assist each other to accomplish our God-given assignments in the earth, and Father Jehovah is faithful to supply us with the support we need.

That is why I constantly ask myself the question, where is my spiritual fight with the whole armor of God? (Ephesians 6:11 NKJV) Some people are very quick to fight with their physical body parts especially their tongue which is the most lethal of them all (Proverbs 18:21 NKJV). What about our spirit man who is strong in God? So shall they fear the name of the Lord from the west, and His glory from the rising of the sun. When the enemy comes in like a flood then the Spirit of the Lord will raise up a standard against him (Isaiah 59:19 NKJV). The Kingdom of Heaven suffers violence and the violent take it by force (Matthew 11:12). I will not allow the enemy to rob me of my inheritance so I am the violent one that will take it without backing down from claiming what is already mine. I know

Conclusion

my authority in Christ Jesus, and the demonic realm is going to know my name like Paul and Jesus in the Bible (Acts 19:15). The enemy must cease and desist right now by the power of my authority to decree and declare him powerless. My Kingdom access pass is already sealed in the mighty name of Jesus which I acquired when He sacrificed His life for humanity. I conquer now because Jesus conquered. I am authorized now because Jesus gained the highest authority of all. I walk in freedom now because Jesus bought my freedom with His blood. Hallelujah! That is a shouting moment alone because Jesus died so I will not have to go without anything lacking, missing, or broken in my life. I will not allow the enemy (father of lies) (John 8:44) and his minions (fallen angels) (2nd Peter 2:4) to have the last laugh or final authority in my life. I will not be deceived with tremendous burdens of emotional despair knowing that Jesus paid it all for me. I must believe, receive, and achieve the promises that Father God made me so I can triumph in my relationships. So if the Son sets you free, you will be free indeed (John 8:36 ESV). God bless you on a victorious healing journey!

About The Author

LaCarrie K. Ojong was born in Chicago, Illinois. She was raised there until she was nine years old, then her single mother decided to move to the twin cities (St. Paul/Minneapolis) area in Minnesota. LaCarrie K. Ojong was raised there from 5th grade through high school, and she always had a passion for participating in creative writing, acting, dancing, and singing projects. She moved to New Orleans, Louisiana, in Spring 2002 and attended Xavier University for a year with a major in accounting. However, LaCarrie decided that accounting was not for her, so she decided to move back to Minnesota at the end of 2002.

She always had a feeling that a healthcare position was the career path she was supposed to be pursuing in her life. So LaCarrie stayed there until 2004, when she and her family decided to move back to Chicago, Illinois. LaCarrie had her son in 2005 and worked as a home health caregiver and a school bus attendant until she decided to go to school to attain her certification in the billing and coding industry in 2007.

About The Author

LaCarrie worked in the medical billing and coding field for 12 years while attaining her Associates of Applied Science degree in Health Information Technology with the hopes of advancing her career. After considering moving to Texas and praying to Father God about raising her son in a better environment, He led her to Franklin, Tennessee in 2014, by faith without knowing anyone there. She continued to work in the medical billing and coding industry until 2017, when she was laid off. During all that time, she felt like she should have gone to school for nursing, which was missing from her life. LaCarrie decided it was now or never to pursue her calling, and it was the right time to complete a nursing degree.

LaCarrie enrolled in Middle Tennessee State University in Murfreesboro, Tennessee, during Fall 2017 to complete her prerequisites, and she was accepted into their nursing program in Fall 2018. She completed her Bachelor of Science in Nursing in December 2020 in the pandemic. LaCarrie is currently working as a neonatal nurse in the NICU unit at Monroe Carell Jr. Children's Hospital at Vanderbilt in Nashville, Tennessee. She currently lives in Murfreesboro, Tennessee, with her son, who is a sophomore in high school.

Index

A

abandonment, 14
Abel, 2
ability, 4, 28, 81
absent, 5, 56
abundance, 50, 53, 67
accountable, 41
accusatory, 69
achieving, 2, 20, 22
addictive thoughts, 57
adolescent, 9
adulthood, 9
affection, 30, 57
afraid, 59
Africa, 12
agenda, 21
agony, 57
agriculture, 12
Alpha, 45

Index

ambition, 33, 67
America, 12
ancestry, 13
anger, 2, 18, 47
anointing, 52, 66
anxious, 32
argue, 56
arrangements, 21
ashamed, 21, 58
ashes, 47
assignments, 27, 31, 82
atmosphere, 22, 43, 48
attitude, 9, 14, 35, 49
attitudes, 33
attractive, 33, 52
attributes, 32, 33, 79
authority, 4, 31, 38, 53, 83
avocado seed, 67

B

babysitting, 8
baggage, 35
bandages, 48
basketball player, 8
beauty, 47, 62
believe, 4, 12, 19, 25, 28, 29, 36, 42, 44, 50, 56, 77, 83
benefits, 20, 23, 32, 34
best friend, 17, 55
Betrayal, 59, 60

Bible, 1, 2, 37, 39, 48, 55, 82, 83

bicycling trail, 77

biological father, 5

birth certificate, 11

bitterness, 11, 24, 48, 60, 64

blessed, 28, 31, 45, 55, 66

blessing, 24, 44, 48, 50, 59

blessings jar, 43

blinded, 47, 60

blueprint, 7, 25

bondage, 4, 53

boo, 56

bottomless pit, 63

boy, 17, 20, 34

boyfriend, 16, 20

Boyfriend, 18

bride, 31, 67

brokenhearted, 50

brokenness, 15, 16, 53

burden, 8, 24, 50, 59

business, 67

C

Cain, 2

camp, 26

career, 43, 84, 85

careers, 20, 43

caregiver, 66, 84

cavalry, 51

Index

chain, 52, 60
challenge, 30
chaos, 23, 49
character, 24, 32, 33, 37, 38, 50, 61
cheap, 21
cheating, 21
cheer, 16
cherub, 81
chest, 7
Chicago, 84
child, 6, 7, 8, 19, 20, 21, 23, 34, 66
children, 3, 6, 7, 8, 13, 20, 35, 39, 40, 44, 82
choice, 3, 22, 26, 43
chore, 20
Christian, 30, 36, 37, 38, 40, 41
chromosomes, 23
church, 31
clock, 58
clothing, 11, 36
coding field, 85
college degree, 12
combative, 69
comfort, 16, 22
Comforter, 55
commandment, 45
commitment level, 34
communication, 7, 9, 10
Communication, 19
compromise, 24, 41
conceited, 61

conceived, 5
conclusion, 29, 64
condemnation, 51
confused, 10
confusion, 27, 39
connection, 3, 11, 14, 17, 26, 34, 37, 38, 58
conquerors, 4
consequences, 2, 18
conversation, 3, 7, 9, 24, 36
corruptible seeds, 26
cost, 21
counselor, 77
country, 12
couple, 19, 20, 23, 65
courage, 6, 48, 57
courtship, 39
covenant, 31, 39, 41
crab meat, 32
crazy, 20, 62
creativity, 66
criticism, 13
crying, 30, 57
curses, 18
cymbal, 48

D

damage, 15, 34, 48
daughter, 6, 8, 38, 67
days, 25, 55

deadline, 54
dealbreaker, 21
deceitful, 37, 43
deceive, 27, 41
deceptive, 22, 37, 57, 60
decision, 4, 5, 21, 22, 26, 30, 31
declaration, 40
declare, 11, 14, 18, 22, 23, 43, 46, 52, 55, 81, 83
decree, 11, 14, 18, 22, 23, 43, 46, 52, 55, 83
defeat, 3, 43, 64
deficits, 15, 50
delivered, 11, 44
demographic, 29
demonic realm, 83
denominator, 15
departures, 24
desires, 34, 35, 37
desolation, 64
desperation, 63
destination point, 44
destiny, 29, 52, 66
deterrence, 26
deuces, 57
devaluing, 57
devastated, 20
devotions, 58
dictate, 29, 30, 48
disappointment, 11, 24, 47
discern, 32, 50, 55
discerning, 3

discontentment, 46
discord, 40
discouraged, 43
discrepancies, 26
disheartening, 11
dismantled, 18
disobedience, 44
disregarded, 24, 35, 48
disrespect, 58
disrespected, 24
disrespectful, 33, 39
distracted, 26, 45
distraction, 41
division, 40
divorce, 5, 28
DNA, 14
domino effect, 17
doubt, 44, 59, 68
drama, 23, 61
dreams, 38, 61
drug store, 34
dysfunctional, 17

E

ear, 61
earth, 1, 25, 31, 34, 45, 52, 66, 82
earthly vessel, 31
educator, 66
emotions, 2, 4, 18, 32, 34, 36, 49, 53, 58, 63, 71, 79

empowering, 16
empty, 32
encourage, 8, 39, 40, 52
encouragement, 13
endeavors, 21
endless cycle, 18
enemy, 3, 25, 26, 27, 33, 37, 40, 41, 43, 49, 50, 51, 52, 53, 54, 55, 81, 82, 83
energy, 35
engagement, 33, 39
engagement period, 33
enlightening, 16
enriching, 16
entrepreneur, 67
envied, 15
environment, 24, 50, 85
equation, 13
eternal damnation, 27
eternity, 23, 28
evil, 25, 42, 43, 50, 81
ex, 42, 77
excuses, 35, 57
exhausted, 27
explanation, 10
eyes, 3, 37, 50, 52, 61, 64

F

Facebook, 12
failure, 22, 52, 53

fair, 23, 26, 60, 65
faith, 21, 29, 30, 40, 50, 54, 66, 67, 68, 81, 85
faithful, 21, 28, 38, 81, 82
fallen angels, 27, 83
familiar spirits, 40
family, 5, 12, 13, 14, 19, 20, 21, 34, 39, 45, 48, 84
Fantasies, 65
fantasy, 22, 29
Father God, 1, 2, 3, 4, 14, 16, 18, 22, 25, 26, 27, 28, 29, 30, 31, 32, 33, 35, 36, 37, 38, 39, 40, 41, 42, 43, 44, 45, 47, 48, 49, 50, 51, 52, 53, 54, 55, 66, 67, 68, 81, 82, 83, 85
fault, 27
favor, 19, 29, 40, 52
fear, 16, 21, 22, 29, 43, 52, 53, 82
fearful, 29
female, 6
financially unstable, 32
fire, 60, 68
food, 11, 56
forgiveness, 67, 81
foundation, 4, 15, 22, 51, 53
Franklin, 85
freedom, 9, 68, 81, 83
friend, 16, 18, 20, 33, 34, 60, 62, 66, 77
friends, 9, 10, 15, 16, 17, 37, 81
friendship, 14, 16, 17, 37
friendships, 15, 17
fruits, 22, 27, 32, 51, 66
frustration, 2, 24, 47
fun, 6, 8, 9, 15, 24

Index

future, 6, 19, 20, 21, 22, 23, 29, 51, 52, 53, 75

G

gentleness, 27
girl, 21, 34, 60, 63
girlfriend, 34, 62
glorify, 66
glory, 22, 28, 35, 40, 42, 43, 45, 48, 51, 54, 68, 82
goal, 22, 29, 50, 54
goals, 33, 79
godly, 77
good listener, 60
good news, 67
goodness, 27, 42, 50
gorgeous, 63, 66
grace, 25, 45, 48, 53, 67, 81
grades, 8
grandmother, 45
grateful, 11, 23, 43
green light, 36
guidance, 10, 44, 45, 52, 54, 68
gym, 36, 77

H

half-truths, 41
handsome, 36
happy, 6, 22
hare, 27

healthcare, 43, 44, 84

healthy, 10, 15, 19, 21, 34, 35, 39, 42, 55, 58, 81

heart, 7, 15, 18, 20, 24, 29, 30, 33, 36, 37, 40, 41, 42, 44, 45, 48, 49, 53, 57, 58, 60, 61, 63, 64, 65, 68, 79

heaven, 25, 27, 45

heavenly Father, 1, 2, 3, 18, 22, 26, 38, 43, 44, 45, 49, 50, 66

Heavenly Father, 50, 52, 54, 68

heavy burden, 35, 42

help, 3, 8, 30, 31, 39, 49, 50, 77, 82

Helper, 55

helpless, 7

hesitation, 44

High Priest, 46

high school, 8, 43, 44, 84, 85

history, 17

Holy Spirit, 28, 40, 55, 67, 68

homebound, 62

homeless, 67

honesty, 21

honor, 11, 51, 54

hoops, 58

hope, 24, 58, 64

hostility, 18

hours, 25, 77

house, 8, 9, 20, 22, 38

household, 5, 7, 19, 21

housing, 11

humanity, 83

humble, 48

hunger, 50

hurt, 3, 9, 11, 17, 24, 25, 34, 35, 49, 60, 63, 69, 71, 73, 75, 81
hurt,, 24
husband, 19, 22, 29, 30, 31, 34, 36, 37, 38, 39, 40, 41

I

ideas, 33
identity, 5, 11, 24, 25, 66
idiotic decision, 2
ignorance, 13, 49
illegal money, 39
Illinois, 84
illusion, 63
imagination, 47
imitation, 32
immature, 19
immaturity, 44, 53
impact, 15, 18, 71, 73
impatient, 1, 31, 32
imperative, 2, 23
imperfections, 3
impossible, 28, 52, 68
inadequacies, 25
incomplete, 32, 65
incompleteness, 14
independence, 20, 34
infectious disease, 49
inheritance, 82
inner knowing, 23
insecurities, 60

insecurity, 11
inspiration, 6
integrity, 14, 24, 38, 41
intelligence, 23, 66
intentions, 24, 34
internal healing, 50
internal issues, 4
intimacy, 60
intoxicating, 30, 58
intuition, 23
invisible, 31
invitation, 4, 65
isolation, 64

J

jealous, 39
jealousy, 2
Jesus, 1, 3, 11, 23, 25, 26, 27, 31, 33, 36, 38, 46, 47, 49, 51, 53, 55, 67, 83
Jesus Christ, 1, 3, 11, 23, 25, 27, 31, 46, 51
job, 19, 36, 42, 43
joker, 26
joking, 6
journey, 2, 4, 20, 22, 26, 30, 33, 44, 50, 51, 53, 54, 83
joy, 18, 27, 49

K

kill, 49

kindness, 20, 27
Kingdom of God, 31, 33
Kingdom of Light, 67
knowledge, 3, 6, 13, 30, 45, 47, 48

L

labor, 19, 32
LaCarrie K. Ojong, 84
lady, 56
laughing, 6
leader, 40, 48
learner, 67
legacy, 45
legs, 7
letters, 4, 11
levels, 19, 60
liars, 26
lie, 3, 28, 29, 40, 41
life, 1, 2, 3, 4, 5, 6, 8, 11, 13, 15, 16, 17, 18, 19, 20, 22, 23, 24, 25, 26, 27, 28, 29, 30, 31, 33, 34, 35, 37, 39, 40, 41, 42, 43, 44, 45, 47, 48, 49, 50, 52, 53, 54, 55, 56, 60, 64, 66, 67, 68, 75, 81, 82, 83, 84, 85
lifestyle, 20, 33
lifetime, 2, 3, 36, 39, 41, 48, 51
lonely, 31
Lord, 1, 25, 29, 31, 49, 53, 55, 82
Louisiana, 84
love, 27, 29, 30, 31, 32, 36, 47, 49, 51, 53, 58, 59, 60, 61, 62, 65, 77, 81

loyalty, 21
luxury car, 36
lying, 57

M

Maker, 55
male, 34
man, 28, 29, 30, 31, 34, 35, 36, 37, 38, 39, 40, 41, 42, 82
manipulation, 63
marriage, 10, 12, 13, 20, 22, 28, 29, 30, 31, 33, 34, 38, 39, 40, 41, 54
married, 5, 22, 28, 29, 31, 40
masterpiece, 51
materialistic, 20
maturity, 14, 34
Maya Angelou, 2
medical billing, 85
memories, 11, 17, 57
mental games, 57
mental state, 42
mentor, 66
mercy, 48, 67
methodology, 54
milestone, 54
mind, 1, 4, 8, 9, 25, 26, 37, 38, 41, 57, 62, 63, 65
mindful, 26, 41
mini-image, 6
minions, 27, 83
ministry, 55

Minneapolis, 84
Minnesota, 84
minutes, 25, 58
misconception, 9
miserable, 44
misleading voices, 55
mission, 24
mistake, 10
mold, 48, 51
money, 12, 33, 34, 39, 42
Monroe Carell Jr. Children's Hospital, 85
months, 25
moody, 15
morals, 24, 33
Most-High, 66, 67
mother, 5, 6, 11, 12, 15, 20, 22, 31, 66, 84
motivation, 20
motives, 31, 37
mountains, 4
mouth, 11, 40, 55
mouthpiece, 67
movies, 30
Murfreesboro, 85

N

Nashville, 85
nations, 67
navigator, 26
neonatal nurse, 85

New Orleans, 84
new wine, 52
Nigeria, 12, 13
Nursing, 43, 85
nursing degree, 85
nursing field, 43, 44

O

obedient, 22, 30, 67
obstacles, 26, 63
offense, 9, 15, 35, 48
old nature, 26, 68
old wineskin, 52
Omega, 45
opinion, 10, 11, 59
opportunity, 4, 7, 10, 22, 50, 51, 65
opposition, 82
oppressor, 31
originator, 3
outcomes, 4, 26, 28, 60
overcomer, 4
overflow, 43

P

pain, 2, 17, 24, 58, 60, 71
pandemic, 85
paralyzed, 21, 52, 63
parents, 7, 14, 21, 23

Index

partnership, 19

passion, 6, 84

pastor, 77

Paul, 83, 84

paycheck, 19

peace, 4, 14, 18, 22, 24, 25, 27, 39, 42, 49, 51

peaceful, 6, 61, 73

peacemakers, 40

personality, 6, 14, 26, 53

personality traits, 14, 53

phone, 12, 13, 14

photos, 11

planet, 29

plans, 20, 21, 33, 36, 44, 49, 50, 51

pleasant, 35, 36

poem, 57

poems, 4

poison, 48

portable CD player, 36

power, 2, 4, 20, 23, 25, 27, 28, 31, 35, 45, 52, 55, 64, 68, 83

praise, 8, 15, 54

pray, 45, 48, 50

prayer life, 33, 45

prayer warrior, 40, 67

prayers, 4, 40, 45

praying, 38, 45, 59, 85

predictable, 57

pregnant, 5

presence, 6, 30, 50, 52, 54

preteen, 9

prey, 40
pride, 46, 60
priesthood, 68
priorities, 34
priority mail, 67
prison, 52
profit, 42
progression, 26
promise, 4, 62
prosperity, 67
protection, 33, 45, 53, 81
protective check, 22
Provider, 41
provision, 41
purpose, 1, 2, 25, 32, 35, 45, 49, 50, 51, 53, 67
puzzle pieces, 5

R

reap, 35, 43
rebellion, 27
red flag, 21
refuse, 43
regret, 23, 53
rejection, 17, 18
relationship, 1, 9, 11, 14, 15, 18, 19, 20, 21, 22, 23, 31, 34, 35, 39, 40, 50, 51, 56, 62, 69, 81
relationships, 1, 2, 3, 4, 6, 7, 10, 15, 16, 19, 24, 25, 26, 35, 39, 48, 49, 50, 51, 52, 53, 60, 71, 73, 75, 79, 81, 83
relatives, 12

relentless, 57
relief, 48
remembrance, 55
remorse, 24
repercussions, 41
research, 28, 43
resentfulness, 15
resolution, 69, 75
resource, 28, 33, 39, 66
responsibility, 3, 8, 14, 20, 33
restoration, 53, 60
restore, 43
retreating, 75
revenge, 24, 75
righteousness, 49, 50, 54
romantic, 1, 7, 19, 30, 37, 38, 40
romanticism, 30
root, 15, 42, 48
royal heir, 67

S

sad, 11
Sam the Provider, 20
sanctuary, 63
satan, 26, 28
Savior, 1, 31, 53
scorpions,, 25
seasons, 3, 45, 50, 52, 54
seconds, 25

secrets, 62
secure, 9, 20, 41
self-control, 27
self-esteem, 18
self-evaluation, 4
self-indulgent, 15
selfish, 3, 6, 8, 12, 15, 22, 23, 30, 31, 32, 34, 35, 37, 39
selfish mentality, 34
selfishness, 33, 46
selflessness, 32
self-reliant, 10
serpents, 25, 38
sevenfold, 43
sex, 10, 19, 41
sexual relations, 33
sexually charged, 32
shame, 13, 23
sheep, 55
Shepherd, 55
shoulders, 7
shy, 13, 65
siblings, 8, 13
singing, 15, 20, 84
sister, 67
Society, 28, 29
son, 9, 21, 22, 23, 84, 85
sophomore, 8, 85
sorrow, 2, 25, 53, 64
soul, 37, 38, 42, 46, 64, 65
soulmate, 37, 64

souls, 18, 37, 38
sow, 35
spa, 77
spectrum, 33
spirit of lust, 33
spirit of righteousness, 48
spiritual birthright, 67
spiritual confirmation, 32
spiritual death, 27, 41, 49
spiritual discernment, 55
spiritual warfare, 67
spouse, 31, 36, 40
stagnation, 26, 52
stomach, 7
story, 12, 13, 31
straight path, 54
stranger, 55
strategies, 50, 64
street, 12
strength, 28, 45, 48, 54, 64, 66, 82
stress, 27, 42, 57, 77
stubborn, 35
student, 13, 67
student visa, 13
submitted, 48
succeed, 1, 42
sun, 82
superhero, 6
supernatural, 52
support, 8, 9, 15, 82

supportive, 15, 60

surrendered, 46

Suzy the Homemaker, 19

T

tantrum, 34

tea, 62

teach, 55, 59

teachings, 6

teenage, 9, 15, 22

tempt, 26

temptation, 32, 41

Tennessee, 85

Texas, 85

texting, 34

therapist, 77

thieves, 17

thirst, 50

toddler, 12

tongue, 82

tortoise, 27, 28

toxic, 18, 25, 34, 49, 50, 81

track team, 8

transformed, 4, 46

transforms, 42

transition period, 45

treasure, 59

trials, 3

tribulations, 3

triumph, 3, 25, 43, 49, 53, 68, 83
triumphant, 51, 81
trouble, 1, 9, 23, 43
truth, 3, 11, 27, 28, 29, 40, 41, 49, 51, 55, 67
two-car garage, 20

U

ugly, 30
unappreciated, 31, 58
unaware, 15, 54
unawareness, 24
unforgiveness, 15, 47, 48
United States, 13
universe, 52
unloved, 31, 58
unnoticed, 31
unselfishly, 57
unwanted, 31
unworthiness, 23
Upgrade U, 20
upset, 14

V

values, 33, 39, 59
vicious sting, 18
victory, 27, 51, 54, 60, 63
vindictiveness, 18
violence, 82

virtuous, 65
vision, 19, 33
vows, 33
vulnerable, 41, 65

W

waist, 7, 61
walking, 32, 38, 77
weak, 57
weary, 54
wedding song, 61
weeks, 25
wellbeing, 15, 26, 34
white dove, 63
wicked, 27, 37, 40, 49
wife, 19, 21, 29, 31, 33, 36, 40, 41
wisdom, 4, 6, 44, 48, 49, 53, 59, 66
wise, 38
witchcraft, 40
woman, 6, 7, 11, 28, 30, 31, 36, 37, 38, 39, 40, 41, 62, 65, 66
working woman, 6
world, 8, 14, 17, 28, 40, 48, 55, 67
wounded, 14, 49
woundedness, 15
wounds, 48, 50
wrath, 60

X

Xavier University, 84

Y

years, 9, 11, 13, 17, 21, 25, 35, 44, 53, 61, 66, 84, 85
yoke, 52

Pain Produces Triumph

www.ingramcontent.com/pod-product-compliance
Lightning Source LLC
Chambersburg PA
CBHW072040110526
44592CB00012B/1493